Praise for *T*

The NLP Professional is a unique book fi   n
the NLP world. Because of her inclusiv   l-
anced and objective views of the curre   es
this refreshingly objective stance with :   al
is written from the heart of a mind wit   :ll
worth your attention.
Joe & Melody Cheal, NLP Master Trainers, The GWiz Learning Partnership

The NLP Professional is a perfect book for every level of NLP training from new starters through to experienced Masters. For a team to be ultimately successful it must be professional at its core and in the individual components. A bad player can produce bad results or end up with bad headlines, great players flow and work almost as one to achieve fantastic results.

This book is just a small part of the legacy that Karen brings to the field. I've witnessed the blood, sweat, tears and hours she has poured into projects. From the conferences, awards, support groups and projects to raise standards for NLP and how bringing together diverse, strong-willed and eclectic individuals and organisations has been for the good of us all and ultimately for the world in which we can help them be the difference that makes the difference. Karen is at the heart of NLP.
Andy Coley CTC Ltd, International NLP Trainer, TedX Speaker & Coach

Karen's timely new edition to the already delightful *The NLP Professional* isn't just recommended reading for NLP professionals but for anyone with an interest in NLP and in being more professional (in this new world of online and hybrid working) in general.

Her open heart, warmth, good humour, common sense and extensive experience offer gorgeous guidance and encouragement to people at different stages of their journeys with NLP and in practice.
Eve Menezes Cunningham, author of *365 Ways to Feel Better: Self-care Ideas for Embodied Wellbeing*

This wonderfully updated version of *The NLP Professional* is both an inspiration and a challenge to all of us in the field.

What does it mean to be a Professional? How do we actually walk our talk? How do we build the credibility that we need in order to make what we do both relevant and meaningful to the challenges that we face in the 21st Century? How can NLP Professionals help make a difference in the World we live in and build thriving practices in an ethical way?

Karen Falconer is a true beacon of light in our profession and I can honestly that say without her guidance and the clear values and ethics that shine through her work and that of ANLP, I would not have had the confidence and the sure platform that our professional body provides to do so much of the work that we do and I whole heartedly recommend this new edition of *The NLP Professional* to anyone who is serious about our field and who wants to use their expertise in NLP to help make a difference in our society.
Michael Dunlop, CEO Power Of Choice Ltd, International Ambassador & Specialist Envoy For Government for ANLP

Karen is synonymous with professionalism and as CEO of ANLP is the perfect person to have written this book – with words of wisdom, great tips, guidance, recommendations and personal stories – she highlights with great flair, how and why you want to be doing NLP super professionally.

If you're starting out with an NLP business – this is a perfect read to support you in setting yourself up in the most professional way from the outset.

If you're already running a good NLP business – this book is reassuring and a reminder of good things to consider, full of great tips and things to review and reflect on.

And if you've been doing this successfully for a while – this book reminds us why we all need to do NLP professionally, whilst also bringing our own style and creativity to the field, so that we can be proud and part of creating something special together.

As Karen reiterates throughout the book, doing this together professionally, not only enables success for everyone but most importantly drives the momentum for the bigger picture; a better world for everyone.

Thank you Karen for facilitating this for us all.
Yvonne Fernando, NLP Master Practitioner & Life Coach

The NLP Professional deals with the issues of the wonderful model of NLP with all its flaws and potentials in the free market. It gives you insight about NLP, and how to apply NLP for an NLP business.

It is a must read for anyone who wants to use NLP in a professional context. As a Director of an international NLP Association ANLP (one of the few established and good reputation Associations) for years, handling all the professional NLP members, Karen knows what is necessary to build and maintain an NLP business successfully as NLP trainer, NLP coach or in therapy.

This book is practical and helpful for anyone who wants to use NLP professionally.
Bert Feustel, NLP Master Trainer, Co-Founder DVNLP, INLPTA Director, Mindsystems, Munich

The unusual titles 'NLP Practitioner' and 'NLP Master' for short trainings of 10 to 18 days each can only be understood historically. What in the 80's of the last century was a cheeky mockery of the traditional education system, today leads to the NLP trainings being labelled 'lightweight' by the education establishment. A 'Master's' degree with less than 150 hours of training, of course, is ridiculous.

The focus on 'professionalism' which Karen Falconer introduces in this not only entertaining to read but above all very inspiring book, shows a (professional) way out of this historical impasse.
Ueli R. Frischknecht, Secretary General IANLP (www.ia-nlp.org)

Would you like to create a Professional NLP Business? If so, what would that require? For answers look no further than this succinct book, *The NLP Professional*. Here, Karen Falconer, the Managing Director of ANLP, has answered these questions and identified the strategy you will need, here you will find both the requisite skills and attitude.

Yet the book offers more than that. Here you will learn about what a *professional attitude* involves, the personal qualities of a true professional, and how *NLP itself* can be more professional as a field. For the person new to the field of NLP, this book offers an excellent way to determine who is truly authentic and credible and who is not. It is a book that can help us forge a great future for NLP!

L. Michael Hall, PhD, Neuro-Semantics Executive Director

Karen's book provides a road map for how to be a successful NLP professional. It covers everything from professional attitude to specific activities that you can do to be successful, drawn on her experience in the field and with many NLP Professionals.

We really don't know anything in the field that offers this kind of information in such a readable, clear, and practical format, and it all being in one place – in this book! We'd highly recommend this book for anyone who wants to take their NLP skills into the professional arena and be well prepared and successful.

Tim and Kris Hallbom, NLP Master Trainers and Consultants

What a timely new edition of this important text. Now, more than ever this second edition offers much needed leadership in the development field, in an open and real discussion around professionalism and standards in the field of NLP. The need to be congruent and professional in our own businesses, and in the sharing of NLP as a field, is a central pillar.

Karen seamlessly integrates and models the entire attitude and philosophy of being congruent in NLP, drawing on her many years of leadership through ANLP. The book offers encouragement and inspiration to others to choose the way they practice, and to consider their wider contribution in the world. It is my pleasure to whole heartedly recommend this new edition.

Dr Suzanne Henwood, Independent Consultant, Auckland, New Zealand

The NLP Professional contains lots of practical tips on how to set up and run a professional business, but for me the heart of the book is how Karen breaks down the complex process of becoming professional into easy-to-understand themes. Also by establishing ANLP International as a community interest company with its multitude of services, magazines and journals, and by writing this book, Karen is not only demonstrating her professional credentials, she is helping others to do the same.

James Lawley, Co-developer of Symbolic Modelling using Clean Language

The NLP Professional is a really useful guide for all NLPers, whether they want to create a successful NLP business or simply to use NLP in a professional manner. The book is full of tips and ideas to take on board, particularly in the early stages of running an NLP-based business. It also raises some essential issues around the development and professionalisation of the whole NLP field and refers to important prevailing legislation which impacts on everyone running an NLP business.

Mirroring Karen's natural approachable and personable manner, *The NLP Professional* is written in conversational style, full of stories and anecdotes. Regardless of the extent to which you adopt Karen's tips, considering them will help you to clarify and achieve your business and professional goals.

Jeremy Lazarus, Master Trainer of NLP, Director, The Lazarus Consultancy Ltd

The NLP Professional is a welcome and accessible guide to promoting professional integrity and evidence-based high standards in the evolving, global field of NLP.

And the key recommendation here for an individual NLP Practitioner is to centre being competent, compassionate and ethical in their practice.

Additionally, it is a wise and practical insider's guide to building a sustainable and ethical business, from someone who has herself stayed true to her creative vision and community commitments, through all the extraordinary challenges and crises of the past few years.

Karen is always working from core NLP principles and practices about values and relationships – and it shows. This is also an excellent and inspirational account of how to use the tools of NLP itself to create and build your own successful NLP-focussed business. Highly recommended.

Judith Lowe, PPD Learning Ltd, NLP Training Institute, London

The NLP Professional is an informative and practical guide to running an NLP business... and way much more than that! With the NLP approach woven through, it demonstrates the relevance of NLP in the business world, underlining the importance, and indeed the good business sense, of being authentic, professional and ethical. It goes beyond advising how to run an NLP Business, this is good advice for any business in my view. I love the tips and the actions at the end of each chapter – my copy will be festooned with post its!

Florence Madden, NLP Trainer and Author of *The Intention Impact Conundrum* and Co-author of *Everyday NLP*

This is a 'must read' for any NLP Professional. Karen's practical approach gives you the structure to grow your level of professionalism, to see your place within the field and to realise your own personal contribution. She outlines a framework of tips to enhance your success and how to move forward to achieve your outcomes within your NLP business in an ethical and ecological way. I highly recommend you taking the time to read and apply this book; to enable you to become the NLP Professional that the world needs right now. I will be recommending this book to my NLP Practitioners. Thank you Karen for all you do for our profession.

Emma McNally MBA, NLP Trainer, Author and founder of Achieve Your Greatness Ltd, School of NLP

The NLP Professional is a must-read and a catalyst for change in our entrepreneurial journey and our NLP field! It's a step-by-step guide supporting us all in becoming the best version of ourselves and our NLP Business, all the while helping to restore NLP's nobility and enhancing its credibility along the way.

Karen's book nourishes the perfect balance of our soul and ego. It encourages us to serve and make a positive difference in the world, and to achieve our desired success in an effective, professional, structured way. It's filled with clear, concrete examples and powerful metaphors that compel our thinking and empower our actions.

Karen truly embodies what NLP professionalism is. You can see, hear and feel her authenticity, compassion, commitment and congruency.

May you feel as inspired as I am to be Proud and Passionate of NLP and to Rise up, Shine and Succeed, individually and collectively, so that our humanity and our world can benefit of the gifts the best of NLP has to offer. NLP can change the World; this book is a step towards it!

Colette Normandeau, International NLP Master-trainer and Director of L'essentiel in Quebec City, Canada, 'NLP in business' award-winner 2021

When NLP students complete their training, we are asked many questions about setting up in practice, from professional memberships through to ethics and the scope of their work based on their NLP training. In the past, we have answered these questions as best as we can, or pointed them in the right direction for the information.

From this point forward, *The NLP Professional* is the resource we will be recommending. It is full of helpful guidance, suggestions and convincing strategies for new practitioners to set up a successful and professional practice.

However, this book is more than a success guide for new NLP practitioners. It's a revolutionary call to NLP Training Institutes. It challenges us to walk the talk and embrace key professional attitudes.

We must rise to the challenge set out in this book or we will miss out on the opportunity to put NLP Training and practice on to a professional level, where we know it belongs.
Tony Nutley, Director and Trainer at UKCPD

This is a great book for all those working with NLP. It provides a framework and guidance for NLP practitioners to develop a career that is successful, ethical and professionally accountable. Combining these important ideas with the NLP approach and skillset provides a clear route for practitioners to powerfully contribute to the worlds of business, education, performance, coaching and clinical work.
Dr Phil Parker, Do PhD, NLP Master Trainer, Researcher and Designer of the Lightning Process for Chronic Health issues

This is the book that the world needs right now especially if you are thinking of becoming an NLP Professional.

When you are just starting out in the field of NLP, it can be a little confusing. This book not only gives you the clarity you need about where the NLP world is right now, but it also helps you with practical and easily applicable strategies to start your NLP business.

And this will allow you to practice NLP in a way that's sustainable for you and contribute to developing the overall field of NLP to create maximum impact in the world.

Karen from her vast experience has shared what it takes and means to be an honest, skilful, successful, and ethical NLP professional.

And as you become that NLP professional, in the process, you will also change your thinking and mindset that will help you transform all areas of your life.
Nishith Shah, Founder of Thought Labs, ANLP Ambassador for India

The NLP Professional by Karen Falconer is a must-read for anyone who dreams of becoming a professional coach as well as for those who already have experience in the coaching business and wish to take it to the next level. This accessible and captivating book, containing plenty of information and experience, will provide many tips, advisory suggestions, and strategies to any reader.

Written in a 'chatty' style and enriched with numerous stories and anecdotes it is an easy read and a practical guide to becoming a genuinely successful professional. I am truly excited to endorse it.

Slavica Squire, NLP Master Trainer, Vice-president of European-Coaching Association (ECA), Master Certified Coach (ICF) and founder of the NLP Institute, Belgrade

Karen has already probably done more than most people to promote high ethical standards and professionalism amongst practitioners of NLP. This book is another manifestation of that commitment. It's one thing to talk about integrity and authenticity, and quite another to model and communicate them in such a down-to-earth way.

Fortunately, it is very evident this book is based not just on Karen's passionate beliefs about how to create a better world, but also on her ability to practise what she preaches; it is encouraging to know that the person who speaks to you here from the printed page is so congruent with the professional code she describes.

Paul Tosey, PhD, Independent Consultant

The world of NLP is indeed broad and varied. Karen Falconer's passionate and utterly professional leadership of ANLP is a shining beacon for both NLP Practitioners of all levels who aim to practice ethically and professionally and also, importantly, for the public; who otherwise may find it a challenging field to navigate and discern.

In this new edition of *The NLP Professional*, Karen surpasses the outstanding first edition and brings it bang up-to-date; not only wholly supportive, but also entirely relevant to the challenges NLP Practitioners and the public (their prospective clients and students) face right now, in our complex and changing world.

Mostly, I highly recommend this book because in it, Karen provides really practical actions to build your business sustainably and to continue your professional development. Karen walks her talk as an NLP Professional impeccably, congruently and consistently. This book is the 'how to' for all of us to raise our own standards and I urge anyone with an interest in NLP to get their copy today and keep it close at hand.

Reb Veale, INLPTA NLP Master Trainer, ANLP Ambassador for France, Director Reveal Solutions Training

THE NLP PROFESSIONAL

Your Future in NLP

Karen Falconer

Published by McNidder & Grace
21 Bridge Street
Carmarthen SA31 3JS
Wales, United Kingdom

www.mcnidderandgrace.com
New edition paperback 2022
© Karen Falconer
First published 2011 by Ecademy Press

ISBN: 9780857162083
Ebook: 9780857162090

Designed by JS Typesetting Ltd, Porthcawl
Cover design: Tabitha Palmer

Printed and bound by Short Run Press Ltd, Exeter, UK

In memory of my Dad, the most consummate professional
I have ever known and an inspirational role model

"Ask not what your country can do for you – ask what you can do for your country."

John F Kennedy, inaugural address

NLP pro·fes·sion·all prə ˈfɛʃ(ə)n(ə)l

A practitioner* of NLP who is serious about their business and who wants to make a difference by delivering their NLP services in a responsible, congruent and ethical way

*practitioner in this sense is anyone who holds an NLP certification, from Diploma to Master Trainer.

Contents

Foreword

It is a great pleasure for us to write this Foreword to the new edition of *The NLP Professional*. If there is anyone who knows both the benefits and challenges of building a business based on NLP, it is Karen Falconer.

The principles and practices that she has chosen to focus on are keys that can open so many professional doors, if consistently applied. They are also the fruits of her experience. We can testify to their effectiveness, both in our own careers and those of our many graduates.

The themes that Karen has written about can be used to build successful businesses of all types and sizes. Karen, for instance, has put time, care and energy into fostering the most successful international NLP Conference in the world. This requires a lot of practical skill and the ability to collaborate effectively with others. It is also driven by a passionate vision of what NLP can offer and fueled by a "how to" generosity: to qualify for inclusion, every workshop must provide people with tools that they can use.

Being a "professional" is ultimately a mindset that drives the practices that Karen has identified. These are exactly the ones needed to create a successful business based on NLP, especially when you care about making a difference. We know because we have done it – be it creating International Teaching Seminars (ITS) in the case of Ian or NLP University (NLPU) in the case of Robert.

Karen advises us to "be curious and be open to the possibilities that might arise when you explore potential avenues for working collaboratively." These are wise words. We speak from experience because we have been doing this for over a quarter of a century. Some of our most rewarding and generative initiatives have come from working together, instead of alone. NLP itself began as a collaborative effort. In addition, the evolution of NLP has grown from addressing individual concerns and issues to resolving collective challenges and fostering collective intelligence.

In our view, being a professional means being both rigorous and inclusive. NLP has always been based on the rigorous evaluation of any approach, tool or technique using a very simple question: "Does it work?" If it does, NLP wants to understand how it works and to let other people know so that it can become part of the human repository of "best practices". This is precisely what Karen has done with this book. She has given us a practical guide to becoming a successful professional, not only in NLP but in any legitimate business.

There is another important take-away, perhaps the most important of all. As she says early on, it's about "being congruent with what you do." We have often had the experience of participants in NLP trainings with us thinking NLP will help them be more effective with other people only to discover that they themselves are the first and primary beneficiaries. This makes sense to us because in our experience you must first engage with yourself before you can effectively engage with others. It's fitting then that towards the end of the book, Karen reminds us of Gandhi's famous dictum, "Be the change you want to see in the world."

Sometimes people think that "how to's" are just techniques, but the how to's that Karen presents are life skills. If we choose to live by these practices, we could end up with more than just a successful business; we might just move in the direction of a life well lived.

Ian McDermott and Robert Dilts
March 2022

Preface

So, what qualifies me to write *The NLP Professional*?

Professionalism can be an attitude, a mindset, a belief, a value. In fact, professionalism can be applied to every level of Dilts logical levels…and for me, professionalism is part of my core identity. My Dad was a criminal solicitor, so from an early age, I was immersed in and mindful of the ways he behaved to maintain his professionalism. Of course, I know now that NLP is about modelling excellence, and growing up in this environment, I was unconsciously modelling his professionalism from an early age! This book is based upon those observed attributes of professionalism, which have been broken down into simple strategies.

After graduating University with a degree in Genetics, I worked in the field of Accountancy for the next 20 years – an already established profession. I discovered NLP and completed my own training over a number of years, realising what a powerful, empowering set of tools were now at my fingertips. When the opportunity came up to take on the Association for NLP (ANLP), I believed I could make a difference.

I have been leading the Association since 2005, and I do, therefore, have a slightly different perspective on the field of NLP. At ANLP, our role is twofold – to represent the views of our members and also to provide information and knowledge to the public about NLP, which means we talk to both NLP professionals and the public on a daily basis, often acting as the bridge between the two.

ANLP LEADERSHIP MODEL

Clients

Professionals

Trainers

ANLP

Governing
Body

Trainers

Professionals

End Users

CLASSIC LEADERSHIP MODEL

ANLP have a powerful and unusual leadership model, which flips the more usual leadership model on its head and promotes a more supportive and empowering style of leadership for the NLP Community.

Sometimes, I think we (ANLP) are the 'empowering connections facilitators' and that our aim is to create an environment that increases the possibility of linking people who have a need with people who have a solution, by presenting the case for 'good NLP'. Our aim is to be the global flagbearers for professional NLP. We hold the space for the NLP Community, and there is a deliberate ambiguity in our strapline, 'Empowering NLP Professionals'…because we do and you are!

Since I took over the Association in 2005, ANLP has evolved into the strong, independent and impartial social enterprise that it is today. In 2008, ANLP became a Community Interest Company, which has certain additional regulations. These also ensure we continue to achieve our main aim, which is to serve the NLP Community. That year, we also co-hosted the first International Research Conference at the University of Surrey.

In 2009, ANLP was awarded the title Small Business of the Year by Hertfordshire Business Awards and I was honoured to receive the award for Hertfordshire Woman of the Year. In 2010, we launched the journal *Current Research in NLP* at the House of Commons, and by 2013, we had hosted two further research conferences and published the corresponding proceedings from those conferences.

In 2016, we were invited to become custodians of the NLP Conference (NLP International Conference, 2016) and continue to host the conference in May each year. The NLP Awards (NLP Awards, 2017) were also introduced during the 2017 conference and have now become an annual celebratory event in the NLP calendar.

In 2020, the pandemic struck, and the whole NLP community learned the value of flexibility and adaptation. ANLP responded by collaborating with the NLP community to create virtual training criteria (ANLP Criteria for Virtual Training, 2020) and provided support and resources for key workers and others struggling with the far-reaching effects of the pandemic. The same year, ANLP was awarded Best UK Community Interest Company in the UK Enterprise Awards.

It was this most recent turn of events that led to a realisation it was time to revise this book. Times have moved on and so has NLP in some ways, and less so in others, which makes this book even more relevant now.

Introduction

Do you want to create a more professional, effective and success-ful NLP business? Would you like more clarity around how to shape your future in NLP?

If you answered 'yes', then this may be the reason you have picked up this book.

'The difference that makes a difference' is one of the first things we learn to look for when we are taught about modelling excellence. Discovering this can make the difference between 'good' and 'great', 'pass' and 'distinction' or even 'success' and 'more feedback' (because as we know, there is no failure, only feedback).

NLP can often be the difference that does make the difference. NLP can be the catalyst which alters someone's perception enough for them to make the changes they desire.

So as NLP Professionals, we are catalyst that change, and this means we can have a positive social impact on society. The challenge can be that although *we* know we can do this, NLP is still not always recognised as a credible and viable option.

NLP continues to evolve and is now at a crossroads, and we, as NLP Professionals, do hold its future in our hands. We collectively have the choice to raise our game and take those next steps towards getting NLP universally recognised as a credible and complemen-tary option. There are other options, and sometimes, it does seem easier to do nothing and let things run their natural course…and this is a choice.

So, what exactly constitutes a 'Professional'? There are two definitions of professional (Oxford Online Dictionary, 2022) we would aspire to meet as NLP Professionals:

1. A person competent or skilled in a particular activity.

2. A person engaged in a specified activity as a main paid occupation rather than as a pastime.

The NLP Professional is about considering the field of NLP as a professional one. It is about making connections between your actions as a practitioner of NLP and considering how these could possibly impact upon your business and the professional field of NLP.

The NLP Professional is about looking at NLP from a different perspective – it is about chunking up and considering NLP as a field of practices, applying perceptual positions and some of the useful tools and techniques we have learned to the field of NLP, and collectively accepting responsibility for taking NLP to the next level.

This book will question practices still prevalent in our field and challenge whether these are ultimately useful if our desired outcome is to raise the profile of NLP and create a profession that has credibility, respect and recognition, and which can stand proudly alongside other helping professions. This *is* your future in NLP.

The title of this book, *The NLP Professional*, is purposeful because I believe there is a distinct difference between an 'NLP practitioner' and an 'NLP Professional'. I make this distinction throughout the book. At the beginning of each chapter, I highlight the differences, of how an NLP practitioner and an NLP Professional will approach topics from different perspective.

NLP is unregulated, so organisations such as ANLP do not have regulatory powers because there is no requirement or obligation to belong to one. Other regulated professions, such as the medical profession, have a requirement that all practising doctors have to belong to the General Medical Council (GMC). The Solicitors Regulation Authority (SRA) follows a similar model for solicitors.

Without regulations in place for NLP; associations can only guide, advise and recommend.

In the absence of regulation, in the field of NLP, adopting the attitude, mindset and habits of professionalism will make a difference.

My desired outcome for writing this book is that you will feel more confident about having a professional, effective and successful NLP business. Ultimately, the more success you have as an NLP Professional, the more people will benefit from the positive applications of NLP.

I want you to be proud of being an NLP Professional and be happy to stand up and be recognised for the NLP skills you offer and the empowering changes you can make to the lives of others.

I will offer you some practical steps and some ideas and perspectives which may help you to reflect upon the part we all have to play in ensuring a bright future for the field of NLP, because ultimately, the success of NLP leads to your success as an NLP Professional.

When you read this book, you will have some different perspectives and reframes to use to develop your practice as an NLP Professional; you will have a greater understanding on how to take action to raise the awareness of NLP; and you will understand the impact you have on creating a positive and successful future for NLP, which ultimately has a positive impact on your NLP business.

After all, ultimately, we are all part of the difference that makes a difference, and so we can all influence how the field of NLP develops.

I wrote this book because I am passionate about NLP, and I strongly believe NLP is one of those personal development philosophies which really can have a positive impact and therefore can make a difference... to an individual, to a team and to society as a whole.

The challenge we face is that there are more and more 'sub-standard' NLP practitioners in the NLP field, mainly due to the online courses, which provide an NLP practitioner certificate in exchange for watching 12 hours worth of online videos! There is no interaction with a real live trainer, there is little or no opportunity to ask questions, explore options or even practice in person... and no opportunity for the student's competence to be assessed before being awarded a certificate.

NLP is rising in popularity and yet still unheard of by many. I believe one of the things that is becoming more significant is the importance of our professionalism in our field. Working together towards becoming a more professionally recognised field will play a key role in ensuring NLP has a strong and positive future.

My first encounter with NLP was when I did a five-week 'Introductory course in Neuro-Linguistic-Programming' at Barnet College. At the time, I had no idea what 'Neuro-Linguistic-Programming' was, and I thought it was either something to do with personal development, something to do with computer programming... or both. As I had an interest in both subjects, and it was only a five-week course, I had nothing to lose by signing up.

It is said you can pinpoint those times in your life that are turning points, and discovering NLP at an evening class in Barnet was definitely one of mine. I had always been interested in personal development, had read my fair share of books and attended workshops...and found that however good my intentions whilst I was immersed in the subject, I seemed to forget all about these wonderful self-development tools I had learned about once I was back in the real world.

NLP is different. There is something uniquely empowering about NLP that has stayed with me and really did enable me to make lasting, sustainable changes to my life. In fact, one of the main reasons I chose to follow up my introductory course with a Practitioner course was because somebody had mentioned 'NLP was one of the few things which had made a lasting difference to my life'. If this was going to be the case, then it seemed like a good investment at the time.

I was sceptical, as my background included a scientific degree and a 20-year career as a management accountant. Could something as simple as altering the appearance of an image in my head (by changing the submodalities) *really* make *that* much difference to the way I handled a particularly challenging person, let's call her Caroline, in my life? It could, and it did, and it still does… and has resulted in a more positive, healthy and sustainable relationship with Caroline.

Before I took over the Association, I spent my days empowering small businesses to take more responsibility for their accounts and develop a greater awareness of their financial situation. By doing this, they were able to make more informed decisions more quickly and more successfully. I was using my own NLP skills daily to improve the effectiveness of my one-to-one training, as well as doing some additional coaching alongside this.

In 2005, I was approached by my former NLP Trainer and asked whether if I was still pursuing my dream – the one I had shared some years earlier when I was the demo subject on my own Practitioner training. My dream had been to create a centre where like-minded people could congregate and share ideas and work together to support each other so they were empowered to make an even bigger difference in society using NLP and coaching.

I had been pursuing my dream in my spare time, but from a completely different angle, and so when I was offered the opportunity to take over ANLP, I paid off the debts of the Association and found myself the proud owner of a one-page website, the ANLP domain name, a magazine which had all but ceased production and a membership list.

I do realise now what a controversial decision I had made – and I am really glad now I made this decision. Early on, there were many times when I really did feel like I had bitten off more than I could chew, and what carried me through those tough times was my belief that NLP is an empowering and potentially life-changing philosophy which can make a positive difference to the lives of others.

Furthermore, I believe if there could be 500 or 5,000 or even 50,000 NLP Practitioners making a difference because of the support they have from ANLP, then together, we would be making a far bigger difference to society than I could ever hope to achieve on my own.

You may be wondering what continues to drive me and spur me into taking action – why is it so important to me that NLP becomes accepted as a credible, professional solution to some of the challenges life can throw at us?

The answer is simple: I know NLP works and does make a difference!

I have experienced the positive impact of NLP for myself, and it really has been *the difference that has made the difference* to my life. As a result, I would love NLP to become a more easily recognised and mainstream solution to the challenges we experience in our lives.

Martin Luther King had an aspirational dream, to overcome barriers and inspire a generation. No matter the size or scope of the dream we all have 'a' dream.

My dream is for NLP to become more widely recognised so it is embraced by society as a solution to many of life's challenges… and as a result, it is embraced by the education system. This, I believe, would mean that young people are given a greater opportunity to benefit from NLP, reach their full potential and be set up for success in the future.

I have watched both my children struggle with the education system for different reasons, and I am driven by my personal experiences and the attitude of many educational establishments I come into contact with.

If NLP was a more acceptable and widely recognised solution in the education system, then Local Government would recognise the positive impact of NLP, young people would benefit from experiencing NLP-based soft skills, would have an even better start in life, achieve their full potential and be set up for success – rather than the current system, which is driven by data, targets and academic achievement and favours those young people who can more easily conform to the system.

Of course, this would have a ripple effect across society. When these empowered young people left school, they would take their NLP skills into their communities and workplaces, and very quickly, within a generation, NLP would become more widely recognised in all areas of society…which is when we start having a much bigger impact on governments, global relationships and conflict resolution.

Whilst this may not be your reason for wanting NLP to become more widely accepted in society, I am betting there is some reason aligned with helping others that brought you into NLP in the first place. So I am guessing you too have your own reasons for wanting NLP to be a more widely embraced option for people seeking solutions to their challenges.

I do also want to reassure you this book is not about standardising NLP and making it so process driven that the flair and flexibility is lost. It is more about how we can work within the parameters of existing society whilst maintaining the flexibility which drives NLP to continually evolve and create a mindset where we can have both creativity and professionalism in the field of NLP.

Finally, whilst I was born and raised in the UK and have spent all my working life here, this book is written to inform anyone wanting to be more professional in their NLP business and in their working lives anywhere on the planet! My only caveat is to make sure that any of the tips and techniques you may wish to use are congruent within the country where you are practising and that you follow and adhere to all local laws and legislation.

CHAPTER 1

Adopting a Professional Attitude

'By the time I was 22, I was a professional. A young and
flawed professional, but not an amateur.'
Stephen Sondheim, composer

Why would you want to adopt a professional attitude in your line
of work? And what exactly is a professional attitude?

Too many practitioners of NLP never consider the impact of their
attitude on their business. It doesn't always occur to them that their
own appearance and the way they present themselves (personally
and professionally) may influence the number of clients they have
or the level of fees they can charge.

As an NLP Professional, you understand that if you want people
to pay good money for your services, you need to look, sound and
feel like you are worth the investment on every level. To borrow a
well-used phrase, 'your attitude determines your altitude.' So in
order to encourage people to part with their money for your services, it is important for you to have a professional attitude.

Attitude is something that NLP practitioners find easy to adopt.
Even if we are not yet engaged in NLP as our main paid occupation
rather than a pastime, we can *act as if* we are. People are more likely
to engage with us if we are acting in a professional way, because this
gives them confidence in our ability.

Being a professional means outwardly demonstrating you have the skills and ability to meet the needs of your potential clients. If you are serious about your NLP business, then I strongly encourage you to treat it like a profession and behave like a Professional.

Of course, NLP is partly about fun and learning in a relaxed and enjoyable environment…and if you want to make a career out of your NLP, there are some elements of this game it would be wise to take seriously. Remember, it is possible to have a professional attitude, run a successful business and enjoy yourself, and I know many NLP Trainers who do successfully combine all three elements. I certainly do, and 'Fun' is one of the ANLP Team's work values!

It is all very well stating that a professional attitude is necessary… and what constitutes a professional attitude and how could you go about achieving a more professional approach to your business?

Creating well-formed outcomes – the business plan

As NLP practitioners, we already know all the benefits of creating some well-formed outcomes and having some CLEAR, PURE and/ or SMART goals defined. And maybe, sometimes, we forget to apply these things to our own business. One of the things I learnt is there is always a good time to make a business plan, however long your business has been running.

All professionals know the value of a business plan, and all effective businesses have a strategic plan. This plan can be a written record defining where we want our business to go and is very much a 'big chunk', meta view of where we want to go. It is always a good idea to start with the end in mind: e.g. where do you want to be in three years' time? After all, if you want to get from London to Paris, there are many different ways to get there and even differing modes of transport, from trains to planes! How you intend to achieve these plans will naturally follow, broken down into smaller, more manageable steps and will be flexible depending on all the things you encounter along the way. Who knows, you may not end up in Paris, and at least, with a strategic plan in place, you will be making a conscious decision to change direction and head for Barcelona instead! (I know, this sounds familiar to you already.)

Schools are a prime example of having a good working model from which they operate. On top of the layers of existing policies and procedures they have, almost every school has an annual School Improvement Plan (SIP), also known as a School Development Plan (SDP). This plan specifically outlines what goals they wish to achieve in the coming year, how they will achieve these, who is responsible for ensuring they are achieved and what the key timed deadlines are for success and achieving various steps along the way.

This is a great model for success and maybe we could take some of these planning models and apply them to our own business.

The book *Enough?* (Armson, 2016) has encouraged my business partner and I to do a lot more future financial planning recently. It has really drawn our attention to future opportunities that we can look forward to if we plan now. We have dedicated a fair bit of time to filling out the spreadsheets provided, making it very comforting to be able to plan various 'what if' scenarios for our future – and to know that we have options!

Like every good plan, there does need to be some flexibility. NLP coach Tim Gunning has two rules for planning:

1. There should always be a plan.
2. Nothing ever goes according to plan.

I use these rules simply to remind myself a certain amount of flexibility is required when running a small business.

So even though, as a small business, you may require a great deal of flexibility, having a business plan really can make a difference. I know it is partly thanks to our business plans and well-formed outcomes that we were rewarded by winning two awards at the Hertfordshire Business Awards in 2009 and Best UK Community Interest Company at the UK Enterprise Awards in 2020.

TIP

Use the boiler plate template provided in the Resources section, which provides you with a starting point for creating your own plan.

I view our business plan a bit like embarking on a water ride or flume at the swimming pool. Our plan is the course we take so we can get from the top of the water ride to the bottom (which usually involves arriving in a pool of water with a big splash). Along the way, we may veer off course slightly and slip from side to side as we rush down the water slides, and yet the sides keep us on course enough to reach our destination – landing with a big splash at the end of the journey…and we've had some fun along the way.

There are times when the importance of having a plan is obvious, and we don't set out without one. Many years ago, my family had the honour and privilege of being able to build our own family home. And I would never have even started this project if we, as a family, hadn't had a plan for executing this project and a set of plans from which to build.

Yet even with a set of plans, we did have to adapt, deviate slightly and make changes along the way. The foundations had to be deeper in one area because we discovered, once we started digging, that the ground structure varied from one end of the plot to the other. We changed the internal layout dramatically before we started building and then made further alterations along the way, once we saw the rooms actually taking shape. The kitchen layout probably changed at least 20 times before we ordered the units. The whole plan, from start to finish, became one big project that, in hindsight, utilised so many of the NLP strategies we all know and understand. I'm pretty sure too that we tested all the presuppositions of NLP along the way:

- The map is not the territory (and neither were the room sizes once we actually laid them out).

- There is no failure, only feedback (how many times did we lay out little paper cut-outs of kitchen units before we had a layout we were all happy with?).

- We all have the resources we need (especially at midnight, when we just needed a bit more energy to finish painting the kitchen before we went to bed).

- Respect for another person's model of the world (it's very important to remember this when dealing with council planning departments and conservation officers, who have rules and by-laws that sometimes make little sense to the rest of us!).

...one cannot *not* communicate (except with plumbers who fail to turn up on site...and even then, there are ways).

The benefits of having a plan could be the difference that makes a difference for your business. Certainly, as far as the house was concerned, having a plan was the one thing that drove us on to completing the project because we were all very clear, as a family, about what we were aiming for, and we were constantly able to remind ourselves of the ultimate goal. (Living in a caravan on site may have helped with the motivation as well).

I'm sure we have all experienced times in the past when we have set out to do something without having any real plan – we'll go with the flow, see where this takes us – and this works really well if we don't have a specific outcome or intention.

I love going out on a Sunday afternoon and just driving somewhere – heading north (or south, east or west), turning left (or right), taking this narrow lane and having the curiosity to see where we end up and what treasures we may discover along the way (usually a tea room, garden centre or simply discovering a stunning view). On the other hand, if I have to be in a particular place at a certain time for a meeting, then my journey is planned – the destination is programmed into my car's satnav, journey times checked (and double checked), and alternative routes planned, and then I'm off.

As far as running my effective business goes, having a plan has been my satnav and has been the difference that makes a difference because the team all know what steps we need to take in order to get us a bit closer to our goals. The plan sometimes acts just as a reminder because we know exactly what we need to be doing; at other times it really does help us to focus and stay on track by guiding us to the next step and reminding us of the bigger picture – the outcome and the reasons for doing what we are doing.

Maintaining a balance

Whilst we may need to use our business plan on occasions to remind ourselves of the bigger picture and the path towards our ultimate outcomes, it is also important to remember to maintain a balance between 'working in' and 'working on' our business.

In case you need to be reminded, 'working in' our business is often what we do best; it's where our area of expertise lies, and it's why we chose to set up our own business in the first place. As a coach or NLP practitioner, you are working 'in' your business when you are working with clients, coaching them or running training courses. You are working 'on' your business when you are working on all other aspects of your business – marketing, administration, planning, continual professional development (CPD) – i.e. all those other aspects of your business which don't directly earn you any money, and which do form a necessary part of the whole business.

Whilst I was working as an accountant, I had a client who had a good balance between working 'in' and 'on' their business. The directors had an eye on the management of the business at the same time as actually contributing to the profitability of the business by working on part-time and lucrative contracts themselves.

On occasions, this balance would waver – when there was a greater demand for contract work and a project was nearing completion, or when the contract work dried up a bit and they could then spend more time planning and structuring their business – and overall, they maintained a balance between the two.

Too much of one or the other can have a detrimental effect on the business. Another client discovered this when their contract work dried up completely for a while, after a period of intense work and pressure. They had been working so hard in their business, they had taken their eye off the bigger picture, i.e. future contracts, and suddenly found themselves with no planned work.

At this point, they panicked, and ended up making some rash short-term decisions – including selling their house – simply because they found themselves quickly moving from a position where they had loads of money coming in, to one where they had very little money coming in.

This same fluctuating cycle can happen with NLP practitioners, who have periods of being really busy with clients and hardly any time to work on the other aspects of their business. After all, when demand is there and client contact hours are very high, the natural tendency is to take all the work offered, just in case. But then, as a skilled NLP Professional, when those clients have all reached their goals, achieved their outcomes and moved on, there follows a quiet period. This often happens because you are so busy working with the clients, you may not have time to do your marketing.

Ideally, it would be great to maintain the balance so even during the busy periods, the marketing wheels are still turning so there is always a steady trickle of new business coming in.

One way to achieve this balance is to schedule in time to work 'on' your business as well as 'in' your business – treat marketing, sales, social media and business development activities as if they were another paying client and schedule them into your diary.

Another thing you can do is decide on your ideal role within your business and work towards this. Do you want to be the hands-on coach because you enjoy working with the clients and helping them? If so, this is what you need to aim for, with most of your time being allocated to clients and employing other people to support you – such as a marketer, administrator and/or bookkeeper – while you are working 'in' your business.

TIP

Set up your business in departments, even if you don't have enough staff to manage each department...yet.

I have applied this tip to ANLP and find it is much easier to manage the business and more clearly define where the most pressing needs are, especially in terms of potentially buying in or delegating services. It also helps the team to know which other departments may need to be involved in projects...even if the departments involved end up only being two people wearing a lot of different hats! It's always good to act 'as if' and adopt the strategies employed by a larger organisation.

Of course, this could be when we sometimes come up against the age-old paradox of balancing time with quality and finances – at some stage, every successful business has dealt with the delicate balancing act between providing high-quality goods or services and finding the time to provide these services and their cost.

In larger organisations, people are employed to focus on specific aspects of the job in order to keep the organisation running smoothly. So a nurse mainly works in the business of caring for patients, i.e. they spend the majority of their day having direct contact with their patients focusing on them. The matron of the ward, on the other hand, spends the majority of their day working on the business of running a ward, managing the staff, the processes and the policies, so having far less direct patient contact. And the hospital administrators, ideally, ensure that the books are balanced and the money is available for both nurse and matron to fulfil their roles.

Even then, it is still vitally important to have the right balance of personnel throughout the organisation – for example, the large secondary school where I was a Governor, was unable to adequately fund admin support, because the bulk of the budget was invested in teaching staff. As a result, the teaching staff became bogged down in photocopying and other admin tasks because there was no admin support for them. Providing admin support would have been better

16

than taking the teachers away from actually teaching! So even in large organisations, there are a few challenges in balancing service provision with the budgets.

Thankfully, we tend to run smaller businesses than in education, and so we have the flexibility to introduce more creative solutions than those employed by Local Government. What creative solutions could you find to ensure you maintain a balance between working 'in' and working 'on' your business? These solutions will differ widely from person to person, and the flexibility comes in utilising whatever works for you and your particular business.

TIP

You probably already have an idea of your financial value in terms of what you charge for your services (by the hour or day). Remember to use your own value when deciding which aspects of your business you could delegate. If your charge out rate is £100 per hour, and a bookkeeper will charge you £30 per hour for dealing with your invoicing and accounts, then where is your time best spent – invoicing or seeing another client?

All the ANLP personnel work virtually and provide us with great services in areas where they have more expertise than I do!

We have several members who use the services of a virtual PA or remote staff, because this frees them up from doing those tedious administrative jobs they do not enjoy and allows them to spend time on the more lucrative aspects of their business. One of them particularly values the work of their virtual administrator because of the freedom this gives her and the opportunities which arise as a result of having some of those administrative tasks taken off her own plate.

On the other hand, a businessman I know views the world very differently. He only employs salespeople, and all staff are expected to focus on how much money they can bring in every month and how much they can contribute to the bottom line. This would work in a large company, where there are other departments to support the sales team, but doesn't seem to work in his small business, because everyone has to work 'in' the business, and there is nobody taking care of any of the other tasks that form part of any successful business, such as administration, marketing and advertising.

Our member who employs the virtual PA is steadily growing her business because she has managed to even out some of the 'in'/'on' fluctuations by effectively sharing her workload. She states that she is now more calm and relaxed and is very happy to delegate certain tasks to ensure they get done and that the business stays on an even keel.

The businessman's company, on the other hand, seems to be more of a rollercoaster ride for everyone involved – which could be fun, I guess, and is probably more stressful. (I say that based on the number of bailiffs who used to turn up looking for payment, because nobody ever had time to settle any bills).

So yes, there is a balance to be found between working 'in' and working 'on' your business, especially if you do want to have an effective one.

TIP

Establish exactly what services you would like to delegate and how you want to use their services. Would you be happy working completely virtually, i.e. no face-to-face contact? Would you prefer some direct contact via the occasional meeting? Or would you prefer to work with someone coming to you on a regular, or irregular, basis, i.e. more freelance administrator rather than virtual services?

The benefit of procedures and 'paperwork'

You are possibly thinking that I am, as a former accountant, a very procedural person in terms of Meta Programs (or Language and Behaviour [LAB] profile). I had better confess now I actually have a heavily options Meta Program, *and* I perceive the value of procedures to be huge because they are a great way to save time and increase efficiency…which enables me to spend far more time doing the things I enjoy doing.

Even as an accountant, I would run through the procedural bit (processing the invoices, balancing the bank account) quickly and easily with the minimum of fuss and effort so I could then get to the bits I enjoyed – the problem-solving bits; the trouble shooting; empowering others by creating some simple processes for them to follow so that their accounts would take them two hours a month rather than two hours a day.

In hindsight, once I had learnt about NLP, I realised a lot of what I was doing with my clients was developing models for them, strategies that would work well for their business and that were broken down enough for them to be able to replicate it – does this sound familiar?

Michael Gerber encourages effective use of procedures and policies in his amazing book *The E-Myth Revisited* (Gerber, 2001). By having processes in place, we are able to delegate tasks to others, whilst still maintaining our sense of what our business is about – the essence of our business. As soon as we have a detailed model for the way our business works, it is very easy for someone else to pick up and complete these tasks on your behalf.

When I first read *The E-Myth Revisited*, I wished I'd read it years ago: I could have saved myself a lot of time and energy. I do believe, though, we come across things when we most need them, and when we are open and ready to receive the wisdom.

So, you can ensure you are running an effective business by having some effective paperwork and processes in place. I'm not talking about NLP processes here; I'm talking about business processes, procedures and policies which you, or anyone you employ, can follow and which will enhance your business efficiency and professionalism.

These processes, procedures and paperwork can be as simple as having a particular strategy for handling a new client. This way, whether you are the person who has the initial contact with your potential client, or it is your virtual PA, your receptionist or your assistant, there is a method, style and strategy for dealing with them. Your efficiency and organisation can have the knock-on effect of demonstrating your professionalism and potentially increasing the confidence your client will have in you.-

How does paperwork come into this? In two ways:

1. Externally improving communications.

   a. Business Cards/Printed Materials

   Imagine what impression your printed materials make, when they may be the first thing that someone sees relating to you, especially with business cards and leaflets being left in the reception areas of health and wellbeing outlets, such as GP surgeries, spas and complementary health establishments.

   Your printed materials may also be the only reminder some-one takes away with them after a business networking meet-ing, or at an exhibition or conference. It may even be that your card or leaflet is passed on to another potential client by someone who thinks they may be interested in your services. So you need your business card to be an informative reminder for your potential client.

   Of course, it is important that your printed materials are relevant to your potential clients. One NLP Trainer I know does a lot of work with corporates, so their printed material is the business card – it works for their potential clients and it's what they expect. Another NLP Professional friend works with individuals and so has both postcards and leaflets to promote various aspects of their work.

Whatever you believe works well for your potential clients, do consider having something that is printed, rather than being totally reliant on your website and social media posts to promote your services. With online print agencies vying for your business, it can be an affordable expense…and you just never know when one of your cards or leaflets may find its way onto the desk of that one important future client.

b. Social Media Touchpoints

Nowadays, a majority of external communication is via social media, so do make sure your Facebook, Twitter, LinkedIn and other social media profiles are attractive and represent the services you can provide.

2. Internally improving business efficiency.

By having special ways of dealing with people and having policies and strategies in place to cover different potential scenarios, you have more chance of appearing confident, competent and professional in the eyes of your potential client.

If you have clear, up-to-date client records and efficient ways of keeping track of your clients, potential clients and ex-clients, you and your colleagues can always handle any calls and queries, because you have clear and simple processes for handling enquiries.

Contrast this with the helpline of a national institution that I had to call three times recently. I needed to know how to update some details, and each time I called the helpline, I was given different advice – and the first two pieces of advice didn't work.

Ideally, a national institution would have a clearly laid out process for changing details, so my query could have been handled efficiently and quickly. Unfortunately, unlike most other small businesses, they do not need to work on winning and retaining customers because we all have to deal with them anyway.

21

Personally, I struggle with the number of different ways I can be contacted nowadays. I know that creating 101 different ways of connecting with the outside world is considered an improvement...and I do find it challenging to keep track of work-related enquiries relayed via letter, phone call, email, Messenger, tweets, LinkedIn messages, voicemail, text and WhatsApp. (I am sure there are more channels, which have passed me by altogether!)

Whether you are using a virtual PA to assist you with running your business or you are managing it on your own right now, I recommend having a strategy for dealing with all communication touchpoints, mainly to ensure you capture them all!

I have learned a lot of different ways over the years for managing my business practices efficiently so I can make the best use of my time. There are some really useful books that offer tips and I have listed these in the Further Reading section.

As a small business, you do need to work on winning and retaining clients, so having systems in place to help you manage your potential and current clients will help.

TIP

There are many customer relationship management (CRM) systems on the market, so just google 'CRM systems' to come up with a multitude of web-based or software systems – you will find at least one to suit your particular requirements.

Another good reason for having an effective set of policies, procedures and paperwork in place is to protect both you and your client. This paperwork can include some basic client information forms, and various checks to ensure you have assessed the appropriateness of taking on this new client as well as a contract to ensure you have some clear boundaries and agreements in place.

Protecting yourself and keeping your clients and potential clients aware of how you keep up with current legislation and best practice surrounding the delivery of your services gives them confidence and should be a given for NLP Professionals. These strategies, procedures and paperwork form another layer of comfort, demonstrating you are a true NLP Professional who knows how to run a business and look after those whom you serve. Yet many NLP practitioners naively dismiss these levels of professionalism, through lack of understanding around the laws that apply to their practices, e.g. Safeguarding Vulnerable Groups Act (SVGA) 2006. Just because NLP is unregulated at the moment does not mean that NLP practitioners are above the law!

I have come across various incidences where having these strategies in place have protected both the client and the NLP practitioner. Whilst delivering a Practitioner training, NLP Trainer Tony Nutley was increasingly concerned about the way a particular student was behaving. Eventually, he felt obliged to ask the student to leave because he was increasingly concerned about the effect this student was having on the other students, the trainers and their assistants.

Tony was able to handle the scenario successfully because he had clear boundaries already in place through a contract and pre-screening forms; he also had policies for recording various observations and incidents and had documented these throughout the course. These procedures benefitted the students because it meant that both successful and unsuccessful students could receive powerful feedback, and that every student had a file documenting their progress throughout the course. Tony also benefitted because his paperwork provided documentary evidence.

Nowadays, with the chances of potential litigation increasing, having procedures and policies in place is something about which insurance companies could become more insistent. In fact, I understand one of the insurance companies which currently covers NLP practitioners will support a claim only if seven years of client notes have been kept by the NLP practitioner. So make sure you read the small print, because they too have policies in place to protect them in the event of a claim.

Presenting yourself as a Professional

Having worked with small and medium businesses since 1988, I have found one of the most important things to take into consideration is to look, sound and feel like a professional on every level. Let's remind ourselves about the VAKOG (visual, auditory, kinaesthetic, gustatory and olfactory) representational systems and how much visual appearance/body language can affect first impressions.

It does vary considerably from person to person, so perhaps, something we can choose to model is the best practice we have seen in other practitioners. One of the things I learned as a management accountant was that looking, sounding and feeling like a professional did not necessarily mean wearing a black suit all the time; it is very much about adapting to your surroundings.

A few years ago I visited a bank with the managing director of a successful media business, who was one of my clients. I was his management accountant and we were going to the bank to ask for a £1 million loan to acquire another company. I turned up to the meeting looking every inch the professional management accountant – black suit, smart shoes, briefcase and reams of supporting paperwork, all professionally produced and neatly filed in a presentation folder. My client turned up wearing a black T-shirt and jeans, and a blazer. I was horrified, because at the time, my model of the world equated professional with a black suit (and there was no flexibility in my model).

I watched my client closely during the presentation (only years later did I appreciate that I was actually running a quick modelling project) and I realised that between us we were presenting a completely professional package. My client may have looked unprofessional in my eyes, and he was very appropriately dressed for a managing director of a media business. What's more, he spoke passionately, he knew his business model inside out, his demeanour oozed confidence – and his resources, i.e. his documents, his business cards and presentation folders (and his accountant) were all profession-ally presented and top quality. Yes, we got the loan.

As former Chair of Trustees (Governors) for our local secondary school, I am very aware of how important it is to dress for the role – I dress very differently for an Ofsted inspection, where I need to give the impression I am an effective School Leader who has some authority and knows what she is talking about, to the outfits I wear for sitting on the Graduation and Referral Committee, where my role is to build rapport with and encourage the young people in Year 7 to be the best they can be. As well as putting at ease the people I am meeting, there is the added benefit of embracing any excuse for a bit of shopping for these outfits!

Of course, presenting yourself as an NLP Professional applies to the virtual world as well. When I found myself conducting *all* my meetings via Zoom during the pandemic, I found that it helped my attitude to dress up rather than down. Whilst the sales of jog-ging bottoms rocketed in 2020, I still wore my professional work clothes to the 'office'! It helped me to get into and maintain my professional attitude, for meetings and general day-to-day running of the business.

As I have alluded to in these examples, professionalism is not just about your personal appearance. It is about every aspect of you which is available in the public domain. So think about what *quality* and *professional* look, sound and feel like to you, because this initial impression, as you know, counts for a lot.

TIP

Think about who you want to engage with in any given meeting and use your appearance to build better rapport and meet your audience in their map of the world.

There are many things you may wish to convey to your potential clients, and somewhere down the line, I'm pretty sure confidence is going to be one of them. Your client will want to feel confident you are the one they can work with; they will want to be confident you have the capability to support them through change; they will want to be confident they are making the right decision.

Part of this confidence will be conveyed to them by how you present yourself and your business. I don't know about you, and I would certainly have more confidence in a dentist who has clean and tidy looking premises, a smiling receptionist with gleaming teeth and the obligatory fish tank in the waiting room…as long as the fish are clean and shiny, like my teeth will be when I'm done.

It is so simple nowadays for anyone to Google you and get your online profile in an instant – so what do these potential links say about you? Do you have the right balance of professional messages and social messages on the internet? If you were to Google your name right now, what would you come up with? Do you have a presence in those professional arenas where you would like to be conducting business? Does your overall social profile present you in a good light?

Be very aware of how easy it is nowadays to get embroiled in personal rants, political views and polarised positioning on social media, which may come back to haunt you in future, partly because of the speed with which debate changes and partly because what you believed 10 years ago may not be what you believe now. Blurring the boundaries between personal views and professional views can backfire as much as it can endear you to your audience, as the article 'Social media profiles that ruined job offers' describes (2022).

From a marketing perspective, remember that people buy people. Certainly in the NLP profession, you are selling your services as an NLP Professional to your potential clients. How do you want people to feel when they have come into contact with you? This is an important aspect of your business because there are emotions involved here – NLP is all about subjective experience. The image you present to the public is the image your potential clients will walk away with.

Are you presenting the image you want to convey to the world (or at least your potential clients)? Think about the tools you use to promote yourself – your business cards, your website, your social media activity, your promotional leaflets. Do they convey the messages you want them to?

For example, how do you deal with phone calls and other auditory means of communication – do you have a dedicated business line at home (so you can convey a professional image rather than have the family picking up your calls)? Do you have an answerphone to pick up messages when you are busy with clients? Do you pay for an answering service to pick up calls in your absence? Or do you rely on your child/partner/dog to entertain your clients until you can get to the phone.

Research indicates that 70% of people do not leave a message on an answerphone, so could this have an impact on your business? We have frequently received feedback suggesting people are relieved when they get to talk to a person and, sometimes, their buying decision will be influenced simply by the fact we answered the phone and they were able to talk to us in person.

TIP

Consider using an answering service to manage your calls – there are many around offering a flexible wide-ranging service and speaking to a real person greatly enhances your ability to connect with your potential clients.

One of the other important things for you to consider, as an NLP Professional, is the location of your business. You have far more flexibility in this respect than some businesses because you are primarily selling your services. Even if you do have products to sell as well, there are now many online outlets to promote these and, sadly, less of a requirement for retail outlets, especially now.

ANLP moved from office premises to all personnel working from home back in 2014, mainly to save on office costs as well as support the environment by cutting down on travel. Of course, the pandemic in 2020 completely revolutionised home working, forcing some sectors to recognise the value of working from home and enable it, as well as creating even more flexible options for NLP Professionals.

And as we adjust to a 'new normal', where working from home is far more acceptable than it was even two years ago, you have so many choices available to you:

Do you work from home, work from office premises, or find another solution? Again, there are pros and cons associated with each option.

If you prefer to work from home, there are some obvious benefits in terms of cost, proximity and convenience. Basing yourself at home is ideal in many respects and do make sure you take everything into consideration.

Where do you want to see your clients? Is there a separate part of your home you can dedicate as a client area? If not, what could a client experience when they come to visit you? Is this the best impression you want to create for them and does this work for them? What is the potential impact on the rest of the family and how does working from home affect your house insurance? Is it a safe enough environment from which to run a one-to-one business – for them and for you?

And how does coaching or training in a virtual environment work for you? Do you have your branding pop up in the background or on a green screen? Do you think about your client's experience when you are fading in and out, merging with your blurred or 'fake' background? Do you have somewhere you can work, without interfering with other home workers, children and pets…or do you simply present yourself authentically to your clients? Luckily, there is now far more tolerance around home working, and unforeseen interruptions just humanise us even more…just like the now infamous BBC TV news interview with Professor Robert Kelly! (Search for 'Children interrupt BBC News interview on YouTube.)

Many practitioners can base themselves at home because they then travel to clients' premises or hire an appropriate workspace when required…or even do their coaching in the garden or whilst walking with their client. Some trainers are now delivering their training virtually, whilst others are going back to the training rooms, or even adopting a hybrid approach.

There are many creative solutions to be found when considering the best 'location' for your business. Just always bear in mind what will work best for your client as well as what works well for you.

TIP

With new meeting spaces popping up virtually and more affordable, flexible in-person options evolving, it really is best to Google what is available in your area.

Summary

I have covered some of the basics about adopting a more professional attitude, and what contributes to the perception of professionalism.

Once you adopt a more professional attitude to your business, you will discover that you can more easily attract the business you are seeking and your NLP business will grow.

When more NLP practitioners adopt a more professional attitude to their business, then NLP as a whole will quickly and easily become recognised as a professional service. And if NLP was more easily recognised as a profession, alongside doctors and lawyers and accountants, then demand for your services will increase and you will increase your client base, making a bigger difference to your own business and to your clients' lives.

So you are already playing a significant part in the field of NLP. Once we all recognise that we have a share in taking responsibility for NLP becoming more widely established as a profession, the ripple effect will take effect and NLP will have a bigger social impact in all our communities…and society as a whole

Actions

Choose one of these areas to work on in the next three months:

- Create or review your business plan.
- Allocate some quality time in your diary to work 'on' your business.
- Review your personal appearance as an NLP Professional and choose one aspect to improve.

Whichever area you choose, make sure you create at least one SMART goal… and email me on admin@anlp. org when you have completed your goal.

CHAPTER 2

Being Congruent
with What You Do

'I challenge you to make your life a masterpiece. I
challenge you to join the ranks of those people who
live what they teach, who walk their talk.'
Tony Robbins, motivational speaker

Authenticity is integrity in action and it is easily detectable – you
don't have to be NLP-trained to work out whether someone is being
congruent (i.e. their values and beliefs match their actions). If a
practitioner of NLP is advocating that their client could use NLP
to improve relationships, or further careers, or overcome fears, or
be a better parent, then it pays to walk the talk and demonstrate
that the practitioner themselves is a living breathing example of the
positive powers of NLP.

As an NLP Professional, you understand how important it is to be
a great ambassador for your business. You recognise that by demonstrating the impact of NLP on their own life, you become the best
possible advert to demonstrate that NLP works.

NLP Professionals understand NLP is about communication, it is
about attitude and it is, in a way, a philosophy for life. You know
you need to make sure you are in the category of people who walk
their talk, rather than insisting: 'Do as I say, not as I do'. You are
a 'centred self' in the NLP community, aware of the role you play

in serving others and making a positive difference to everyone you connect with.

I think I grew up in a world of axioms – among the many I learned as a child were 'walk the talk' and 'practise what you preach', and these have stayed with me over the years.

NLP is about subjective experience, so it does make sense that we need to experience NLP ourselves before we can expect others to do the same. A lot of NLP is also content-free, so even though it is important we experience the practice of NLP, we will all apply this to our own unique issues and challenges, and the results will probably be unique to us.

NLP is about practice and although there are theories which underpin it, it tends to work best when you take action, when you actually do it. As Carl Jung said, 'Children are educated by what the grown-up is and not by his talk.'

Being authentic

If we have experienced NLP for ourselves, in whatever context, we are able to approach our clients from a place of understanding. We do need to have experienced the six-step reframe, anchoring, sub-modalities, perceptual positions and parts integration for ourselves so that we are better placed to act as a guide for our clients to do the same.

Have you ever received one of those emails that promise to teach you the techniques you need to become a millionaire, simply by attending their amazing wealth course? Many years ago, I did and realised quickly that the people running these courses are not actually millionaires themselves! However, it seemed they did know of someone who had made millions following their strategies. So, they were hoping I would take a huge leap of faith and accept their offer to teach me some techniques which they themselves have not successfully put into practice... yet.

I listen to many personal development CDs, and in my opinion, one of the best sets I have ever listened to, was recorded by Gill

Fielding, the wealth expert and millionaire (Fielding, 2008). She knows about creating wealth, she experienced poverty as a child and has become a successful millionaire now.

She is walking her talk and sharing her experiences with others which is real and believable. She has a genuine desire to share her knowledge and guide others along the path she has already travelled.

In this particular instance, I think context and content of her experience (i.e. moving from poverty to wealth) are very important and relevant to what she offers in the set of CDs. However, as an NLP professional, it is the experience of having used NLP on ourselves which is important so that we can demonstrate that we are genuinely walking our talk. This way, we are asking no more of others than we are prepared to do ourselves.

We are taught in NLP that content is rarely relevant. However, sometimes the content can be relevant and end up forming the basis of a niche business, offered as a service to others. NLP Trainer Neil Almond put his own NLP to good effect in very personal circumstances. Neil and his partner Andy were travelling in Australia in 2008, when their small plane crashed. Yes, they really did crash, into the sea – and they all survived. Neil and Andy utilised every NLP skill they could muster to help them overcome this trauma, including:

- Reframing the experience in the moment, to realise how lucky they were to have survived.

- Focusing on a positive outcome.

- Time Line techniques and future pacing.

- Changing the submodalities of the experience.

- Staying at cause.

- Dissociation techniques.

- Moving from victim at identity level by recategorising the experience using Dilts Logical Levels.

- Holding on to the presuppositions of NLP, especially 'we have all the resources we need'.

What I find most incredible and admirable is that Neil and Andy flew back to Australia 12 months later, despite their understandable fears and trepidation. Neil really can now claim to be an expert in overcoming flying phobia; this is his specific niche, the service he can provide.

Neil serialised his experience in *Rapport*, the magazine for NLP Professionals, which has been replicated as a case study on the ANLP website (Almond, 2019).

I'm not suggesting we all need to fully experience the context in which we apply our NLP as Neil did. I'm not going to encourage anyone to take risks (which would be a bit extreme).

What I am suggesting is that in order to fully engage with your client, there does need to be a level of congruence within you which comes from being in a place of understanding. If you are congruent with and believe in what you are doing, your client stands a much better chance of achieving their own outcomes.

If you are asking a client to take a leap of faith and work with you utilising NLP skills and techniques to overcome their challenge, then some real experience of NLP and some understanding of what they are going through to overcome their challenges will help. This is why all NLP training courses do need to have a large element of experiential learning and why NLP just cannot be effectively integrated simply by reading a book or completing a series of pre-recorded videos via an online training platform.

Sometimes we can be unconsciously incongruent within ourselves – in other words, we may not be aware of this incongruence at the time. You will be familiar with Robert Dilts's Logical Levels and how he links environment, behaviours, capabilities, beliefs, values and identity.

Incongruence can arise when there is inner conflict between our own logical levels. Our beliefs can play havoc with our own congruence, especially those beliefs around capabilities.

I remember experiencing this inner conflict when I attended my initial coaching training weekend. We had an inspiring talk on the Sunday afternoon about how to get clients. We were encouraged to take action as soon as possible and start recruiting clients as soon as we got back home, if not before. One of the potential sources for new clients was through networking groups, and we were tasked with joining one of these groups as soon as possible.

I duly searched the internet on Monday morning and found my most local networking group, which met in the golf club at 7 a.m. every Thursday. They had a spare slot for a coach and were delighted to welcome me as a new member.

The inspirational talk I had heard the previous Sunday managed to motivate me until 6.59 a.m. on Thursday morning. The moment I walked into the golf club and was introduced to a suitably suited businessman, I felt completely at home as a management account-ant – and completely out of my depth as a coach.

At the time, I had 15 years' experience as a management account-ant and trainer, compared to the one weekend's training I had re-ceived as prospective coach — and I hadn't even finished reading the coaching manual. Yet there I was, answering questions about coaching, and standing up to deliver a one-minute presentation about what I did for a living, as a coach.

There is 'acting as if' and believing *Yes, I can do this* – yet I felt, in this particular situation, that what I was doing was completely wrong. At the time, I had no experience as a coach apart from one weekend of coaching like-minded people who were attending the same course. I felt very uncomfortable, and I was terrified of actu-ally winning some business as a coach.

In hindsight, I realise my lack of confidence and my incongruence must have been shining through like some sort of warning beacon, clear for all to see, despite my best attempts to 'act as if'. 'Acting as if' only works for me if I believe in what I am doing and have some sort of congruence between my beliefs and my competence.

TIP

Make sure you do have congruence within yourself and that your own beliefs do align with your business, so you can deliver your business messages with authenticity.

I know this now because I can compare this experience with another — and I have been able to work out the difference that made the difference.

When I was on the parents' committee of my son's school, four mums (including myself) had the brilliant idea of raising money for the Meningitis Trust. We wanted to do this because the young daughter of one mum had had meningitis a few months early. She had, thankfully, fully recovered, and it had been an anxious time for all of us.

Right from the start we had the motivation, the drive and the belief we could do this. Our aim was to raise £10,000 for the Meningitis Trust in one day by running one big event.

Nobody believed we could do it; they said we were overstretching ourselves and that our goal was impossible. Even the local Round Table raised only between £6,000 and £7,000 a year at their annual summer fair, and that was an established event being run by a well-known and well-respected local fundraising group. What chance did we possibly have to beat this?

Yet we believed we could do it, and we spent six months acting 'as if' we were running a major event to raise funds for charity. We believed in our cause and we spent hours on the phone and in meetings, talking to local, national and international companies and asking for their support.

We held our event, a fun run and fair, and we raised £13,000 in one day for the Meningitis Trust. Putting this in perspective, in 1994, this was an incredible amount of money to raise at a locally run event, without any social media or fundraising apps that could drawn upon to increase our fundraising activities! We achieved and exceeded our goal because we were all very congruent with what we were doing and our beliefs were fully aligned with our actions.

I share this to emphasise my message that saying one thing and then doing another does send out mixed and confusing messages. And yet, as we know, confusion does seem to lead to a greater under-standing because, quite often, those confusing messages allow us to realise there is some sort of incongruence at play.

I continue to be amazed (or amused?) when I visit health care es-tablishments, like hospitals, and see health care workers standing outside the main entrance smoking. Sometimes, the patients are out there as well (they can be identified as the ones wearing the regulation hospital gowns.). Whatever one's beliefs about the rights and wrongs of smoking, I think most people understand it is bad for one's health…so what sort of mixed message do we get from this scenario?

We discredit the skills of our fellow human beings if we assume they cannot tell when we are being incongruent and not walking our talk. And nowadays (I'm starting to sound 'old' here) with so-cial media, online news and the internet at our fingertips, every incongruent action can be called out, highlighted and discussed in fine detail.

At the moment, one of the incongruent trends being highlighted is the actions of those in the public arena who support environmental causes and yet do little to curtail their own environmentally dam-aging actions – private jets are less than environmentally friendly and create ill feeling when those using them are suggesting that we should be more mindful of the planet.

So in an NLP context, whilst there are some elements of NLP which we would save for utilising for particular challenges or in the train-ing room, there are other elements of NLP we can choose to bring into our own lives, every day, including:

- Values and beliefs.

- The presuppositions of NLP.

- Building rapport.

- Checking ecology.

- Applying perceptual positions.

- Being 'at cause' and taking 100% responsibility.

Values and beliefs

I believe two of the most important values held by NLP Professionals are integrity and trust.

When you start working with a potential client, you are entering into a partnership and relationship with this client. In an NLP Professional's map of the world, integrity and trust are essential to any successful partnership.

Essentially, in a coaching or NLP partnership, we are holding the space for the client to make the changes they want. By holding the space I mean we are giving our clients a safe environment and space (metaphorically and sometimes literally) to be able to explore new possibilities and make changes to their own lives. It is about cause and effect, and us giving them the space to be 'at cause' and take responsibility for themselves, taking the action they deem necessary to get results.

It's a bit like when our children do their homework. When they were younger, I would sit with my sons on homework nights and effectively hold the space for them, so they could focus on taking the right action to complete the required homework. For my younger son especially, who is on the autistic spectrum, this kind of focus could be quite challenging, and it was so tempting sometimes, simply to give him the answers and do his homework for him. However, 95% of the time, I did manage to hold the space for them and allow them to find the answers for themselves…even if this did take an hour longer.

You may have experienced this special and safe environment when you were doing your own NLP training. When I was doing my NLP training, I was lucky enough to find myself with some great people and we were all able to create and hold the space for each other. We were all going through some pretty deep changes ourselves, and there had to be a great deal of trust and integrity between us so we could successfully take those steps for ourselves and deal with our own challenges.

Sometimes, a client does need to have enough trust in you so they can develop the confidence they need to take the required action. Quite often, all it needs is a bit of courage, and to have someone like you, holding the space and creating the safe environment for them to take the step, is what makes the difference.

I remember first getting into the driving seat of a car, ready to learn to drive. My driving instructor talked to me first, explaining exactly what I needed to do, where the safety net was (the dual controls). In hindsight, not only were they trying to ensure our safety I realise that at least a small part of what they were doing was also to build some trust and rapport with me before I set off.

I remember doing all the necessary checks, turning the key and starting the engine, taking the handbrake off, performing mirror, signal, manoeuvre – and then putting my foot on the accelerator for the very first time. The car lurched forward and we gave a very good impression of a kangaroo for the first five minutes or so (I was very relieved we had no audience).

Once I had made those first tentative moves, I then had the confidence to do more, and by the end of the first lesson, thanks to the nurturing and patience of my instructor, I was on my way to becoming a driver.

Many years later, I experienced a whole new level of trust when I took my son and his friend on holiday. They had the opportunity to abseil from a tower, across the lake to an island – and then swing back into the lake before being lowered into a boat and brought back to shore. Easy, especially for adventurous young boys who were keen on Scouts!

The young people, it seemed, were oozing confidence and were keen to give this a go. I played the supportive mum and took them over to the tower, ready to shout words of encouragement as they abseiled into the distance. I had spent the morning building up their enthusiasm and excitement in readiness for the highlight of the holiday.

When we reached the tower, which had seemed quite small from a distance, everything suddenly seemed a whole lot bigger and more daunting. My son turned to me and said, 'You go first'. This hadn't been part of my plan at all, especially as I had various challenges with both heights and letting go, and I found myself at the top of the tower, being strapped into various harnesses and safety equipment and standing on the edge of a very tall platform, looking out over the lake.

My son and his friend were standing at the bottom of the tower, shouting words of encouragement up at me – and reminding me about positive mental attitude and the benefits of trying something new. (Wasn't I supposed to be saying this to them?) As the role model and trusted adult in this situation, I felt I had to walk my own talk, and so I found myself putting a huge amount of trust into the complete stranger who was harnessing me to this very thin rope that appeared to stretch for miles into the distance.

I stood on the edge of the platform for what seemed like ages. The instructor murmured words of encouragement and ran through the safety checks one more time. I put every ounce of faith and trust into him and the safety equipment and I stepped off the platform…and enjoyed moments of complete exhilaration and excitement greater than I have ever experienced before. More importantly, I had done it, I had walked my talk. My son and his friend, who had both put their trust in me, were now prepared to have a go themselves.

TIP

Be prepared to pace and lead your potential clients before they are ready to engage your services (or even those of another NLP Professional). You may know the benefits of what you can do for them…and they may need convincing.

If we are to be completely congruent with what we do and present an air of authenticity, then we do need to have our values and beliefs aligned with what we actually do.

ANLP turns down membership applications from practitioners who don't meet the membership criteria.

It would be so much easier for ANLP to just take their money and accept them. However, that would mean compromising on their values and beliefs around what constitutes an appropriate NLP training course, which will produce well-rounded, informed and capable practitioners.

TIP

If you are feeling uncomfortable working with a particular client, check your values for a potential mismatch. No matter how much you know you can help, if the values don't match, this can play havoc with a relationship. It may even impact upon the results.

The Presuppositions of NLP

The Presuppositions of NLP (Presuppositions of NLP, 2019) form part of the philosophical thinking behind NLP. The presuppositions are designed to give us some useful insights into behaviour and therefore give us greater understanding, and perhaps more tolerance of others.

So once we have an awareness of the presuppositions of NLP, we can apply these to our own lives. If we have embraced NLP in our lives, as well as encouraging others to do the same, then the presuppositions come as part of the package. They are part of the richness which is NLP and underpin it in so many ways.

It took me a while to understand the philosophy behind presuppositions of NLP, because I started off by thinking they would work only if everyone in society adopted them. Of course, as soon as I realised that once I accepted the presuppositions of NLP, my life became easier because they can add meaning and give a useful reframe to explain the behaviour of another person.

TIP

Remember there is no failure, only feedback. One of the most valuable ways you can improve your own business is by accepting feedback as free consultancy advice and being grateful for the opportunity to make positive changes.

Building rapport

It is easier to build rapport with someone when you are genuinely interested in what they have to say, and you do have some empathy with them. Aren't you more likely to engage with a client if you can unconsciously build rapport with them?

Generally, people are more mindful nowadays of building rapport. Once upon a time, the telephone salespeople would simply ask to speak to the managing director, make some comment about the weather and then launch into their spiel about their product or service.

Now, they spend the time attempting to build rapport first: *And how are you today?*, *What are you doing?*, *How could this be made easier for you?*…and *This is how we can help*. Great salespeople have learned to do this naturally and will engage with you and identify your requirements before they sell you their solution.

Sometimes, though, it is easy to work out these salespeople are just going through the motions. They have been given a script and may even have been on a training course. Often, they have been told what they need to do and how to do it, and they are going through the motions, doing their job and consciously attempting to build rapport. However, if our own sensory acuity is triggered and we become acutely aware of this, it could have the opposite effect – i.e. put us off, rather than encouraging us to buy.

I remember being in an interview with someone who clearly had some understanding of rapport and was keen to demonstrate their skills by consciously trying to build rapport with me. Throughout the interview, I was matched and mirrored to within an inch of my life, my every action was copied – and I confess that after an hour of this, I was exhausted. I had become so self-conscious of my own actions, I completely lost the flow of my own thoughts and I felt less able to effectively communicate. Funnily enough, this particular relationship did not go further.

Genuine rapport works wonders – we know it does and it will make a difference to the results you get with your clients. NLP allows us to understand how rapport can work and be used effectively…as long as we are walking our talk and can master this to an extent we are unconsciously competent, or at least doing it mindfully.

Checking ecology

We could make our own lives a lot easier sometimes, by taking a step back to think and plan before we act. We learn about checking ecology on our NLP course, i.e. considering the impact of our intended actions on our existing lifestyle and relationships, and yet sometimes, we do get so caught up in the moment we may lose focus, both on our intended outcome and our own ecology.

NLP Trainer and entrepreneur Emma Sargent wrote a very honest and open piece for *Rapport*, where she admitted their family move from London to the West Country had not exactly gone to plan because they simply hadn't considered all the potential consequences of making such a move. For a while, life was idyllic, and yet her business really suffered and the family had to find far more creative ways to rebuild their business in another part of the UK.

ANLP once received a complaint about an NLP Practitioner from a woman whose boyfriend had undertaken a one-to-one NLP consultation. They didn't know what the original consultation was about, but the result was that the boyfriend packed his bags and left this woman. She wanted to complain about the NLP Practitioner on the basis that she was not happy with the results of her (now ex-) boyfriend's consultation. She felt NLP was to blame.

ANLP had to help her manage her state, and her expectations, as well as to support her in determining that there were some more realistic outcomes that were to blame other than to blame NLP.

It is quite possible that the NLP practitioner did do the ecology checks, and that the client was aware of the potential consequences of his actions that followed his NLP consultation. However, this is a great reminder about the importance of ecology checking and the consequences that may result from the actions that follow, whether, or not, NLP was the catalyst.

Checking ecology applies equally to your own business, and it is important to recognise any potential knock-on effects, or consequences of your actions when building an ecologically sound professional NLP business.

Applying perceptual positions

Perceptual positions is a valuable NLP tool, which has a variety of powerful uses when working with clients. As an NLP Professional, you certainly do not need me to go into the detail of using perceptual positions effectively with clients.

There are many areas where an NLP Professional can also benefit by applying the concept of perceptual positions to their own business. This can be an invaluable way to evaluate aspects of your own business in a more detached and rational way, and review your business from another perspective.

TIP

Use perceptual positions for evaluating your own professionalism and hone in on various aspects of your business. For example:

- What impression do you want clients to get when they look at your online profile?

- What impression do potential clients get when they look at your online profile, and is this the same as the impression you want to convey?

- What would your trusted mentor advise in this situation, so the message you convey aligns with the message your potential clients expect?

Being 'at cause' and taking 100% responsibility

It is important for NLP Professionals to recognise the value of being 'at cause' and acting with responsibility. As an NLP Professional you have been hired to do a job, and this job is usually to support a client in metaphorically moving from where they are now to where they want to be.

Being 'at cause' means stepping up and owning your choices and your actions, especially in a professional arena. Of course, there are occasions when external events do impact on what we are doing – for example, when the internet crashes halfway through a client meeting! We can put contingency plans in place for those things.

For NLP to be successful, it is important that all parties involved embrace the concept of being 'at cause' and accepting 100% responsibility for their actions. When clients are not 'at cause', the result will be 'NLP didn't work'!

Of course, the client takes responsibility for making those changes and taking the action which will move them from A to B, because, ultimately, it is their life and their choice. But as the professional, it is your responsibility to correctly assess the situation and decide on the appropriateness of your actions and interventions, the strategies and models you may choose to introduce to your client.

I had a client who employed me as their management accountant because their previous businesses had failed, due to a variety of reasons including 'rubbish bookkeeper, bad debts, staffing issues'. You name it, their business had suffered from it and all these things had resulted in their previous two businesses going into liquidation.

I did their accounts for a while, and because I kept the accounts accurately, it quickly became apparent the business owner was actually the main drain on the business, because he was continually borrowing the business funds for personal use. Even though I took responsibility and demonstrated this to him, it was not something he was prepared to accept. I stepped away from this client because I realised he was not 'at cause' and was going to be looking for another scapegoat very soon, as his third business began to fail.

Every NLP practitioner may claim that their business has been affected by recession, a lack of clients, others not taking responsibility for promoting NLP widely enough…and at the end of the day, if every one of us takes 100% responsibility for running our own business effectively, we stand a much better chance of succeeding.

Summary

Applying the philosophies, tools, techniques and strategies we learn in NLP to ourselves and our own business can be very relevant. Walking our own talk will lead to us, as NLP Professionals, practising with a greater degree of congruence and authenticity.

By being a great ambassador for your business, you are also acting as a great ambassador for NLP as well as raising awareness around NLP and the positive influence it can have on life.

Actions

- Choose any NLP strategy and apply it to your business. You have plenty to choose from including well-formed outcomes, the presuppositions of NLP, perceptual positions, pacing and leading, cause and effect.
- Re-elicit your business values and prioritise them – check these against both your personal values and your business plan and make sure all aspects align.

CHAPTER 3
Demonstrating Best Practice

**'I do the very best I know how – the very best I can; and
I mean to keep on doing so until the end.'**
Abraham Lincoln

This is the one area many practitioners of NLP shy away from – demonstrating best practice. Many practitioners of NLP feel their creativity could be stifled, and others just want to standardise what NLP has to offer. Some practitioners of NLP simply do not understand what best practice is and have no idea how easy it is to adopt best practice principles for themselves.

NLP Professionals, on the other hand, embrace the opportunity to demonstrate best practice, because it allows them to demonstrate they have an awareness of their responsibility to their clients. Best practice allows you, as a Professional, to accept accountability for your actions and very much puts you at cause with your clients.

In turn, this gives reassurance to your potential clients that you are taking responsibility for your actions and your part in the process of change. Not only is this setting a great example to your clients, it also gives them reassurance that NLP could be a credible solution to their particular issue.

When considering best practice for NLP Professionals, there are various models we could adapt and adopt from other professions, including:

- Scope of practice.

- Ethics in practice.

- Recognising boundaries

- Realistic representation of NLP as a solution.

- Referral systems.

- Coaching, mentoring and supervision.

Scope of practice

As an NLP Professional, it is so important to be aware of your scope of practice, i.e. know what you are capable of handling in a professional situation. However well qualified and experienced a practitioner is, you may not have the right experience to deal with every issue which arises.

When I received my certificate to prove I was an NLP Practitioner, I was excited. Everything I had been working towards came together when I received my NLP Practitioner certificate – and then I stepped out into the real world. What, exactly, did this certification mean? What, specifically, was I capable of doing?

To be honest, when I received my NLP Practitioner certificate, I felt qualified to manage my own life much better than I could some months earlier. In hindsight, I now understand this particular training was designed with this purpose in mind, so I did come out with what I expected, as did everyone else on my course. We all knew and understood we had been enlightened and educated in some really useful strategies for managing our own lives.

The thought of putting 'NLP Practitioner' on my business card briefly crossed my mind...and was instantly dismissed – I had attended a relatively short course in NLP, and my initial outcome for attending the course had been achieved. I had, however, discovered along the way that NLP was immensely powerful and really was making a difference to my life in a way no other personal development training course had done.

I personally did not want to put NLP Practitioner on my business card because I did not feel I was in any way qualified to advertise, let alone practise my NLP on other people. So what, if anything, did I feel comfortable and congruent with saying in order to promote my new training in NLP?

As I became more (un)consciously competent and more confident, I did find I was using my NLP to enhance my work as a management accountant and accounts trainer. The process was subtle and when my accounts clients noticed the difference, I would tell them I was using NLP skills to support them…and that worked for me.

More challenging was what I could call myself, now I had these additional NLP skills!

As CEO of ANLP, one of the questions I am asked by newly qualified practitioners is: 'Am I a therapist now?'

The short answer is no, probably not.

I was very aware that receiving my NLP Practitioner certificate did not qualify me as a therapist of any sort. Given that the dictionary definition of a therapist is 'a person who treats physical, mental or social disorders or disease', and the definition of a practitioner is 'a person who practises a profession or art', there are very few NLP certifications which will automatically qualify anyone as a therapist.

NLP and coaching differ from therapy because they start with a belief the client is OK, well and whole, and simply wants some help moving from where they are now to where they would like to be. Therapy can often be more about delving into the past and exploring things in greater detail, unpicking them so it is possible to understand the impact of past experiences.

As part of a therapeutic journey, it may be that NLP will be used to alter one's view of past events and reframe them in some way so they become more manageable and have less effect on current behaviours, and NLP can be content free, whereas therapists do include references to the specific content.

Another reframe is to look upon therapy and NLP coaching as being presented with a packet of sunflower seeds and a garden which looks ready for planting. NLP and coaching will assume the soil is OK and ready for planting in, and an NLP coach will support the gardener to achieve their dream of having a garden full of sunflowers by next summer.

The therapist will support the gardener to dig over the soil first, take out all the stones, analyse the soil quality and make sure the ground is thoroughly prepared and weed free before planting the seeds.

As a gardener, I know both methods have their place – it is perfectly possible to plant the seeds without any soil preparation and nurture those seeds as they grow, watering them and pulling up the small weeds as they appear. Often, this is all that is needed to achieve a beautiful garden full of sunflowers, because the soil was healthy and ready to grow seeds.

Sometimes, it really doesn't matter how well the seeds are nurtured; the sunflower seeds do not grow tall and straight because there is something lurking in the soil which prevents this from happening. The soil looked fine when the seeds were planted, but something is affecting the progress of the seeds.

Sometimes, NLP and coaching can quite easily deal with the some-thing by clearing the limiting belief or asking powerful questions. And sometimes, regardless of our own and our client's capabilities, we do need to call in the soil expert.

In the case of NLP, these soil experts – i.e. NLP psychotherapists – will have the specialist certifications to handle these cases where additional support is required. Some of the confusion surrounding NLP and whether or not one is qualified as a therapist stems from the modelling projects first undertaken by Richard Bandler and John Grinder when NLP was in its infancy. Bandler and Grinder modelled therapists – Virginia Satir, the psychotherapist responsible for introducing family therapy; Fritz Perls, the psychiatrist and psychotherapist who introduced gestalt therapy; and Milton Erickson, a psychiatrist who had a big influence on hypnosis and family therapy.

Bandler and Grinder used these models to demonstrate that if the strategies used by therapists were broken down into their constituent parts, then it was possible to replicate some of the results achieved by these therapists, i.e. they demonstrated the art of modelling excellence.

It is possible to achieve great results modelling the excellence of therapists and this is what makes NLP so effective in many different areas. NLP has been greatly influenced by the work of these successful therapists and is all about modelling some of the excellent strategies used by therapists in order to achieve results. This is not the same as saying you are a therapist.

There are many other elements which are required in order to qualify as a therapist, in just the same way as there are many other elements required to turn me into as successful a runner as Roger Bannister, the first person to run a sub-4-minute mile. I can model his strategies and work out the 'difference that makes the difference' and this will, I am sure, improve my average times for running a mile. I do also need some other things in order to be at the next Olympics, standing next to the other athletes in the final – peak fitness levels, training and some initial talent would certainly help!

To clarify, I believe, in my role as CEO of ANLP, that obtaining a certificate only qualifies you as an NLP therapist when you have also met the rigorous requirements of United Kingdom Council for Psychotherapy (UKCP), the British Association for Counselling and Psychotherapy (BACP) or the Neuro-Linguistic Psychotherapy and Counselling Association (NLPtCA). Obtaining a bona fide certificate as an NLP Practitioner usually takes somewhere between 50 and 125 hours and will usually include a combination of study and practice (i.e. both knowledge and skills will be measured).

To qualify as an NLP psychotherapist takes over 4 years and includes a combination of training, supervision, client contact, safeguarding and self-directed learning…of which only a small part is achieving both Practitioner and Master Practitioner certifications (UKCP Standards of Education and Training, 2022)

It is perfectly reasonable to add your NLP certification to your existing therapist qualifications, in order to enhance your existing therapeutic practice. I know of many NLP Practitioners who use their NLP to enhance their specific qualifications as a GP, a psychologist, or a psychiatrist, and many others who have undertaken the rigorous training to qualify as an NLP psychotherapist. These people all use their NLP to enhance their existing knowledge and skills and thereby give an even better and more rounded service to their patients.

I have been challenged on the use of the word *therapist* because at ANLP, we encourage our members to position themselves wisely in the marketplace and avoid calling themselves therapists. I agree that in society, the word *therapy* is loosely used to describe a vast array of activities, including retail therapy…in other words, an activity that makes us feel better about ourselves! NLP could definitely fall into that category.

However, the use of the words *therapist* and *therapy* are context specific and we do all know that 'retail therapy' means going shopping. What might be less clear is that when a potential client is looking for support, they may be less aware of the fine distinctions between an NLP psychotherapist and an NLP Professional.

TIP

Instead of using terms like NLP Therapist to describe your role, use NLP Professional, or Educationalist or Consultant, depending on the context of your particular business.

Another question which is frequently debated is: 'Can NLP practitioners ever do harm?'

I know coaching and NLP work on the basic assumption the client is whole and well, rather than broken in any way, and all an NLP Professional needs to do is support them to find the resources they need, and already have within them, in order to make the changes they want to make.

Is this basic assumption *always* true? Does this apply to every client you ever take on? Or is this assumption sometimes a convenient one to make in order to justify the actions of the coach? Is it ever possible to cause harm using NLP or coaching?

These questions were raised at a regulation debate in a coaching forum, and the view was very much that coaching could never cause harm to others. Personally, having given these questions a great deal of thought, I think it is possible to do more harm than good on some occasions with some clients, using both NLP and coaching.

Could it ever be possible to ask a powerful coaching question, which a client continues to deeply process after their coaching session and which could lead to unforeseen consequences after the coaching session has finished?

I took a call into the ANLP office one day, from someone who wanted some help and was not sure what to do or where to go. I assumed this was just another call from someone wanting a list of practitioners in their area, so started down the conversational route, which the ANLP team have quite regularly with callers.

This caller was quite insistent he went to an experienced Master Practitioner because he had already been to see a Practitioner who had successfully dealt with his initial issue. However, as a result of seeing this Practitioner, he had now developed agoraphobia and he wanted to see a more experienced NLP Practitioner in order to get rid of this.

Now, I suspect what had happened in this case is that the caller had some serious underlying issue or traumatic event, deeply hidden in his unconscious, and over the years he had put various strategies in place to effectively deal with this trauma and enable him to get on with life. The NLP Practitioner had successfully helped the client to remove these strategies, at which point the client had to find some new extreme strategies, very quickly, to cover up what had been uncovered…so he became agoraphobic.

This is an extreme example and many people successfully utilise NLP, on a daily basis, to successfully support their clients through change. The point is, it is important to be *aware* of the impact NLP can have and take responsibility for ensuring you use your skills wisely, so that you can support your client to achieve the best possible outcome. Of course, an NLP practitioner may not realise, in the first instance, that there may be underlying issues. This does not change the need for awareness and mindfulness in understanding the power of NLP transformational change.

As an NLP Professional, you will always have a good awareness of your scope of practice and which clients you can realistically take on.

TIP

Be clear about what your own NLP certifications enable you to do in practice. If you would like further clarification, talk to your trainer or contact ANLP for impartial advice.

Ethics in practice

Professional ethics can, on one level, encompass a Code of Ethics, Code of Conduct and Code of Practice… and sometimes all three. A Code of Conduct sets the standard of conduct expected of any professional, regardless of their field of practice. It outlines the behaviour and attitudes that you could expect to experience from anyone who abides by the Code. It guides professionals to provide a minimum standard of client care and support and is viewed as a sign of best practice.

However, within NLP, there are certain additional ethical codes in play, which are relevant and significant in the field of NLP, because we are, by the very nature of our subject, more aware of language. In my opinion, these additional ethics fall broadly into two categories:

- Ethics around misrepresenting certifications.
- Ethics around use of misleading language.

Ethics around misrepresenting certifications

ANLP continues to monitor certification. Every certificate sent to us in support of a membership application is checked and verified… so as far as ANLP membership is concerned, it has never been a case of someone 'paying to belong to the professional body'!

However, what NLP does do well is model the qualification structure used by some other professions and make good use of the language around certification and qualification, which can potentially be misleading and cause confusion, especially with the general public (NLP Certification Structure, 2019).

For example, in NLP, the most basic certification we have is a Diploma – this usually equates to between two and four days' training in NLP and is often a precursor to a full Practitioner training. However, in the higher education system, there is a Higher Diploma in Education, which is achieved after one year full-time or two years' part-time study at a higher education establishment – i.e. University. A qualified teacher can then put 'Dip. Ed' after their name.

Unfortunately, it has been known for holders of a Diploma certificate in NLP to put 'Dip. NLP' after their name. This is a blatant exploitation of the qualifications system and uses a minor certification in NLP to imply something far greater than it really is. Using NLP language in this manipulative way is misleading and does nothing to enhance the reputation of NLP. It is already clearly stated in the ANLP Code of Ethics that this behaviour is unacceptable and would be a breach of the Code of Ethics (ANLP Members Code of Ethics, 2019).

I do know of one NLP Trainer who asked a student to leave his course when he discovered the main reason for them being there was so they could do the minimum amount of training and then use the abbreviation 'Dip. NLP' after their name, to imply a full academic qualification.

We can take this further – once qualified as a Master Practitioner in NLP, I have seen instances where this has been abbreviated to 'Master's'. For example, statements on promotional literature stating 'I have a Master's in NLP' or 'I am qualified to Master's level in NLP'.

Again, within the higher education system, a Master's degree is a post-graduate degree which can be achieved by a number of different routes, and usually involves a further one or two years' study after spending three years as an undergraduate to achieve a first degree.

Compare this to the amount of study time required to become an NLP Master Practitioner – it is possible to achieve a Master Practitioner certificate after only 130 hours of training (50 for Practitioner and 80 for Master Practitioner), and even the most rigorous NLP course will give you a certificate as a Master Practitioner after 300 hours of training (150 each for Practitioner and Master Practitioner). So a Master Practitioner certification equates to between three and seven *weeks* of full-time studying, as opposed to the four or five *years* attending University in order to achieve a Master's degree.

To further add to the confusion, the highest rank of NLP certification is that of a Master Trainer of NLP, which is a level above NLP Trainer. In the NLP field, it is accepted that only bona fide Master Trainers can deliver NLP Trainers training.

Whilst it is laudable that the field of NLP has modelled other qualification systems, this just adds further confusion because in NLP we have two references to the word 'Master' (Master Practitioner and Master Trainer) which are sometimes deliberately interchanged and loosely used to imply the holder has a Master's degree in NLP.

It is also possible to achieve a Master's degree (MSc or MA) from various universities which have an element of NLP and/or coaching included…so these interchangeable references to 'Master's' do allow some practitioners of NLP to misrepresent their certifications to the public, using them to imply something they are not.

It can be easy for an unscrupulous NLP practitioner to misrepresent themselves and their certification, in order to elevate their own credibility.

TIP

Be clear about how you convey your certifications and memberships to your potential clients and ensure you are as transparent as you can be with your own statements.

Ethics around use of misleading language

It seems a few people are willing to go even further in their clever use of language to imply recognition or accreditation by one or more professional body, and thus attempt to further enhance their chances of picking up additional work and new clients. ANLP receive enquiries and complaints about the clever use of wording on various websites. For example:

This course is recognised by ANLP, for membership – technically this is correct, as the course is being delivered by a bona fide NLP Trainer, and any Practitioner course, provided it is delivered by a bona fide certified NLP Trainer and is at least 50 hours, does mean the student is eligible for membership of ANLP. But it is still misleading to state this course is recognised by ANLP, because this wording implies this Trainer has gone through some additional recognition/ accreditation process in order to achieve special recognition.

A N Other is a well-known trainer for ANLP – actually, A N Other is a member of ANLP. They pay their annual membership to belong to the Association; they do not represent ANLP in any training capacity, nor do they train on behalf of ANLP, because ANLP does not run NLP trainings, its members do.

NLP does give us a greater understanding around language and the effects this can have on others. This is where NLP can be viewed as being manipulative because as experts in the field of language, it could be argued any misleading statements made by an NLP practitioner are made intentionally and with full understanding of their intended consequences.

Where the power lies, for an NLP Professional, is in being able to do something with this understanding of language. I know of one NLP Trainer who works with children, and very clearly describes how language can have a negative effect on a child. She tells the story about how a seven-year-old was having problems with their peers and their schoolwork, following the death of their grandfather.

When they were asked what was making schoolwork tricky now, they replied they had lost their confidence…because Mummy had told them they had. Even though they had no idea what confidence was, what it looked, sounded or felt like, being told they had lost confidence was having a huge impact on this child's life.

I experienced something similar when I was in hospital a few years ago. I was due to have an operation which had been scheduled for months and was fairly routine day surgery, which meant I would go into hospital, have the operation and then be allocated a bed in a ward afterwards. So there I sat, in the waiting room, just like a normal GP appointment.

In turn, we each got called in to see our surgeon for a pre-op check. Over the months, I had got well used to putting my own filters in place, I chose to modify the language of the medics before it reached me. So when they told me 'you will get these side effects', I heard 'you *may possibly* get some side effects'. When they listed all the risks of the operation and the anaesthetic, I heard about the *potential* risks.

If only medics fully understood the effects of the language they used. This way, those who don't understand the effect of their language could have been better cushioned in this situation…and more able to enjoy the benefits of approaching their operation with a slightly more positive frame of mind.

Luckily, more Healthcare professionals are receiving training in NLP, thanks to the great work being done by NLP Trainers in the Healthcare sector. There are NLP books specifically tailored to this sector and more case studies referring directly to work done within the NHS (see Further Reading and Resources sections for specific examples).

Thankfully, you, as an NLP Professional, already understand the effects language can have, which is why you will always consider the impact of your claims regarding certifications, experience and achievements, ensuring these are accurately represented and never misleading.

In the long run, this manipulation of language to imply things can backfire, and I have seen an increase in cases being brought by Trading Standards and the Advertising Standards Authority (ASA) when the public complain they are being misled. This does nothing to enhance the reputation of some NLP practitioners or the reputation of NLP. More on this in Chapter 7.

Recognising boundaries

All of us are working within professional, ethical, moral and legislative boundaries, by virtue of the fact we live on this planet!

So, rather than delving too deeply into ethical, moral and legislative boundaries, let's first address the whole debate around potential regulation.

At the moment, despite some websites claims to the contrary, coaching and NLP are unregulated and the debate surrounding potential regulation is a controversial topic.

Some people would question 'Why would anyone want to regulate NLP in the first place?' Well, I have probably already answered this question by illustrating not everyone has the same level of responsibility towards their NLP and coaching practices, in just the same way not everyone has the same attitude towards driving.

Think about it for a moment – when it comes to driving, we are all individuals and across the range there will be some very diverse approaches to driving, with some of us managing to get through our entire driving career without so much as a parking ticket or speeding fine, whereas others may end up being jailed or banned for careless driving…and most of us are somewhere in between.

We do, however, have wide-ranging driving laws in the UK, which are designed to ensure the safety of *every* individual on the road and everyone we may come into contact with whilst on the road. Sometimes, these laws may be perceived as being restrictive or plain ridiculous on occasions, and yet their intention is to protect us – this is the positive intention behind regulation.

The challenge with regulation is that sometimes, in an attempt to protect the public from a few irresponsible individuals, there does sometimes seem to be an extreme response. The challenge at the other end of the spectrum is a system of free for all, where we are left to our own devices and chaos ensues.

The point is that many of our activities and behaviours are already influenced by regulatory boundaries, which we adhere to and re-spect – they do not unduly impact on our daily lives because they are an accepted part of our daily lives.

The important thing to bear in mind, as an NLP Professional, is that even though NLP and coaching are not specifically regulated, as I mentioned previously there are already laws and regulations in place which do affect us as NLP practitioners and which are designed to protect the public.

TIP

Make sure you are working within existing legislation for your area of expertise. In the UK, there is a government website listing all legislation (UK Government Legislation, 2022).

I think it would be a good idea for NLP Practitioners to at least investigate how we could be best prepared for this opportunity. At the moment, regulation for NLP Practitioners is a choice, i.e. there is no specific statutory regulation, so we currently have the opportunity to be curious about the options and explore how we could best work with them.

We have an opportunity to demonstrate, as a profession, we can take responsibility for ourselves and have in place good systems for encouraging self-responsibility. We can demonstrate we already adhere to standards of best practice, we take responsibility for the continued development of our skills, we recognise our scope of practice and we have systems in place to deal with unexpected outcomes.

This way, if regulation is introduced at a later date, because we have demonstrated we are already acting responsibly, any regulation could be more sympathetic with a lighter touch approach, simply because we have demonstrated we already have good self-regulatory systems in place.

Alternatively, NLP practitioners could continue to ignore the possibility of regulation, preferring instead to take a more maverick approach which means they can continue to do what they like and when they like, with no accountability to others.

I believe this is not the case for NLP Professionals and most of us understand that whilst NLP is empowering and enlightens us to the options and choices we have, we are still operating within the basic rules of society and continue to respect this.

As with all laws and regulations, if we are staying within these boundaries anyway, they will not actually affect our practice. If we already have effective self-regulatory boundaries in place, then it is only those who stray from these boundaries who need to be concerned.

There are many laws in the UK, which have no effect on my life whatsoever because my own standards of behaviour mean I am living within those boundaries anyway. It is only when I am straying close to the statutory boundaries (like keeping to the 30-mile limit on an open road), that I then become aware and do need to consciously make the effort to work within the existing regulations.

What is important in any regulation debate is that we have a voice at the table; we have the opportunity to put our point of view across and to be recognised and heard in case the debate about potential regulation starts to become a reality.

I propose therefore, it would be a good idea to be open to greater levels of professionalism and self-regulation in the field of NLP and take steps to get our own house in order. This way, we are prepared for what may (or may not) happen and we have taken steps to demonstrate our own sense of responsibility whilst we do still have a choice in the matter.

The National Autistic Society (NAS) were successful in getting the first specific autism bill, the Autism Act (2009) through parliament, because they were at the table, working with Dame Cheryl Gillan MP, representing their members and their families, and were able to speak with authority about how people with autism are affected in everyday society. As a result, the Autism Act provides a legal duty to provide adult autism services in England.

The same will be true for NLP – when it comes to issues such as regulation, standards and legislation, the 50,000 plus qualified NLP Professionals in the UK are not going to be individually and personally invited, by the government or the potential regulators, to come and have a chat about how regulation could affect them and their business.

What the government and regulators will want to do is engage with the professional bodies and trade associations which represent the views of their members. It is much easier and more practical for them to talk to a small group of people who represent their profession, rather than engage with every person in the profession individually. In fact, the HPC state any profession needs to 'have at least one established professional body which accounts for a significant proportion of that occupational group'.

When the Advertising Standards Authority (ASA) had their remit extended to include websites in 2010 (Advertising Standards Authority Home Page, 2022), there were some legislative implications for practitioners of NLP who do imply or make claims about their competence, because there is now an extra layer of regulation to comply with, especially in the field of health and wellbeing.

The ASA's remit was extended to ensure advertising and marketing materials on websites, as with other advertising, is decent, legal, honest and truthful. In other words, it is recognised that businesses are using misleading language to make various claims, and now the weight of the Government has stepped in to protect the public.

This was actually good news for NLP Professionals, because it meant those practitioners who do make far-reaching claims about their services, do now have an authority to answer to. The downside is many bona fide practitioners of personal development methodologies such as NLP, Coaching and Hypnotherapy find themselves unable to fully promote the success of their services because of the stringent requirements that are now in place.

However, the Committee of Advertising Practice (CAP) were happy to work with ANLP at the time, to provide guidelines for members, because this was a more pragmatic and manageable solution for them, rather than have to deal individually with a number of NLP professionals.

TIP

The ASA regulations do mean testimonials can no longer be used to endorse a claim relating to various medical conditions. Do check their guidelines for what is and isn't allowed in terms of testimonial use (ASA Testimonials and Endorsements, 2022) . If you are a member of ANLP, you can also check the specific CAP guidelines provided for members (ASA Guidelines for ANLP Members, 2019).

Realistic representation of NLP as a solution

NLP can be hugely empowering, especially when we realise we have a choice about our emotions and about how we choose to feel, think and do. NLP can have an important part to play in our lives and in the lives of others.

NLP has a relevant and positive part to play in many health-related situations, and it is not a cure-all. NLP can be effectively used on its own, in many situations and there are times when it can act as a complementary and supportive treatment alongside other, more conventional tools. It is, therefore, really important to be realistic about how and when NLP can be effective.

Any client does need to be willing and ready for NLP to be effective in the first place. However much we want our client to change, whatever benefits we can see for our client, they are the only ones who can take the action and make the necessary changes.

I have taken calls from people asking if NLP will work for them and wanting some sort of guarantee that their issues will be resolved after they have been 'treated with NLP'. As we know, the client does have to be an active and willing participant in the game, rather than a spectator. The NLP Professional is the coach, rather than the player so realistically, it doesn't matter how good you are, if the client isn't engaging with the process, it is less likely to be successful.

Let's face it, fifty per cent of the problem is actually acknowledging there is an issue and taking enough responsibility to do something about it. Courts can send offenders to drug rehabilitation centres and alcoholism clinics, and unless the offender actually takes some responsibility for their own wellbeing, they may well reoffend.

Our home was burgled a few years ago and we actually caught the offender still in the house. He pleaded not guilty for various reasons, and changed his plea when it came to court, and asked for in excess of 80 other offences to be taken into account. It then transpired he also had a large number of previous convictions, most of which were fuelled by his drug habit.

He was given drug rehabilitation again, as well as a custodial sentence, and I wonder, at what point he will choose to follow another path. If he was open to rehabilitation, then NLP could play a valuable part in his recovery, even if it were simply to engage with him for long enough to pace and lead him to a point where he was open to other possibilities.

Referral systems

If NLP were to more closely model best practice adopted by other professions, then NLP practitioners would already have very slick client referral systems in place.

Medical General Practitioners (GPs) have a referral system in place, which they will call upon as soon as their assessment of the situation indicates specialist help is required. We know, and expect, this service from our GP and we trust them, as professionals in their field, to know what they can deal with themselves and what they will refer on to another professional.

As a management accountant and trainer, I knew my scope of practice and area of expertise was in preparing management accounts and training others to do the same. I had initially trained with a firm of accountants, so there was always someone to call upon who knew about the things I didn't.

As my experience grew, I did learn some basics in tax planning, auditing, trusts and strategic planning, and yet, when I became self-employed I was very aware of my boundaries of responsibility and expertise. I knew what I could generally deal with and I knew when I could stretch my boundaries and experience by taking on something which would challenge me, without compromising my clients…and I always had other professionals I could refer my clients on to for specialist advice.

It is so easy for us to sometimes believe we can solve every issue using NLP, and it is completely understandable we would want to, given our desire to help and support our clients.

I once had a conversation with an NLP Practitioner who was excited because they had just been approached by someone who had obsessive compulsive disorder (OCD) and had heard NLP could help.

This Practitioner was enthusiastic and eager to help, newly qualified, had no prior experience with psychological disorders, no knowledge of safeguarding and no system in place for referring on clients who may prove to be a little more challenging than they could cope with.

Despite this, they were going to take on the client because it was 'a useful experience and could be an interesting challenge'. An interesting challenge for whom, exactly? It is one thing for an NLP practitioner to want to stretch themselves and test themselves in challenging situations – after all, how else could they grow and gain new experiences? It is quite another to take on a client presenting something which we know to be outside our scope of practice, with no safety net in place, simply because it could be interesting. Taking on an 'interesting case' without running any ecology checks, supervisory back up or considering the outcome for the client is totally unacceptable and unprofessional behaviour.

When adopting a professional mindset, it is essential to consider whether or not the service you are providing is the best possible service for your client.

TIP

Make it your business to get to know other helping professionals in your area, so you can build your own local database for referring clients.

Coaching, mentoring and supervision

In effect, having your own coach, mentor or supervisor comes back down to walking your talk. If you are proposing your services can support people to make lasting and significant changes to their lives, doesn't it follow you may also need support in your journey as an NLP professional? After all, it is a requirement for many professionals to undertake coaching, mentoring and supervision for themselves so, as NLP Professionals, we model that best practice.

The field of NLP is a subjective one, and by its very nature, could be perceived as 'messing with people's heads'. NLP language is supposed to challenge our thinking patterns and potentially alter our beliefs, opening up new opportunities and choices for future consideration.

You may find at various stages in your NLP career you would benefit from different levels of coaching, mentoring or supervision. I know as a newly qualified practitioner I would have welcomed some mentoring and supervision, so I had someone more experienced than me to share my concerns or client experiences with. I really did feel, on occasions, that I would appreciate the input from someone more experienced to offer guidance and suggestions.

There are many benefits to supervision both for new practitioners and those who have been in the field for many years. Having someone to share challenging experiences with, challenge you and offer quality feedback and hold space for you to be even better at what you do is both a privilege and an essential element of being an NLP Professional. If all your progress is self-monitored, how can you ever be sure there is an element of objectivity?

I currently have an NLP coach and a business mentor, and both provide an invaluable service, enabling me to move forward and holding me to account in just the same way you might do with your own clients. I have, in the past, worked with a qualified Supervisor to ensure I had someone to sanity check my experiences and actions.

TIP

Walk your talk and get your own coach, mentor or supervisor.

Continual professional development

Many professions nowadays recognise the value of undertaking continual professional development (CPD). Certainly, I would suggest in the ever-evolving world of NLP, CPD is a good professional model to adopt and some of the professional bodies, including ANLP, have introduced guidelines.

The essence of NLP is about modelling excellence, and because of this, the field continues to evolve. If you want to deliver the best service possible to your clients, and ensure those models learned about some years previously are still working, it is recommended to continue to professionally develop and refresh your knowledge and skills on a regular basis.

There are different CPD models currently available, and the most commonly recognised one is completing a set number of additional hours training every year. There is a move, however, in some professions, towards reflective learning as a basis for CPD, which is the model adopted by ANLP.

After all, it is possible to turn up at a conference or workshop, obtain a CPD certificate declaring 8 hours' attendance at a conference…and then sit in the coffee bar for three hours before heading back home. (I did do this once because the workshop was, in my opinion, less than good. I hasten to add I did not collect my CPD certificate and never added attendance to my own CPD records.) To be honest, the workshop attendance model works well only if you have a lot of money to spend on additional courses.

The reflective learning model of CPD is far more flexible (you can probably tell I like flexibility). Any form of learning can be incorporated in this model, which means it is far more accessible and affordable for any professional. As its basis is one of reflecting on what you have learned, and how this could impact on your business, your clients, your own self development, then many different learnings can be incorporated in this model – reading a relevant book, attending a practice group, having a useful, educative discussion with a colleague or supervisor. All these activities can be reflected upon and their impact on your business can be measured and recorded.

This model is becoming more recognised and has already been adopted by some of the caring professions such as nurses and radiographers, where it is not simply a question of acquiring more knowledge about the subject, it's also about applying these skills to improve practices. ANLP also model this approach to CPD, and more NLP and coaching training schools are moving towards this standard of practice for NLP.

To quote Peter Drucker, Austrian-American Educator: 'Follow effective action with quiet reflection. From the quiet reflection will come even more effective action.'

TIP

Keep your own knowledge up to date by undertaking regular CPD – this can be as simple as attending a Practice Group or reading a relevant book. Record your reflective observations and how your own behaviours, practices and skills have been enhanced as a result – that is CPD in action.

Professional Standards of Practice

In 2020, in a further drive to improve professionalism in the field, ANLP raised the bar for NLP Professionals by introducing a tangible, evidence-based, professional standards of practice module for their members and reflects many of the practices listed above (How to Apply for Professional Standards, 2020). It was modelled on other professions and their requirements to demonstrate simple elements of professional practice, which would be expected of any professional working with clients or students.

Whether you are a member of ANLP or not, any NLP professional can adopt these professional standards of practice to demonstrate to their clients that they are:

- Appropriately insured.

- Experienced because they see clients/train on a regular basis.

- Continuing to develop themselves professionally through CPD.

- Attending practice groups or peer mentoring to hone their skills.

- Benefitting from regular supervision.

Summary

Modelling best practice from other professions can include an awareness of your scope of practice standards and ethics, realistic representation of NLP as a potential solution, having appropriate referral systems on place, having your own coach, mentor or supervisor and undertaking continual professional development.

As well as increasing your own credibility as an NLP Professional, adopting the principles of best practice will certainly add to the credibility of the field of NLP, which ultimately contributes to NLP being recognised as a credible profession and your demand, as an NLP Professional, increasing as a result.

Actions

- If you haven't already got them, create one-to-one coaching agreements for your clients – these will protect both you and them in the event of any misunderstanding.
- Commit to at least one continual professional development (CPD) activity in the next three months. This can be anything from attending a practice group meeting to booking a business workshop/webinar or reading a relevant book.

CHAPTER 4

Appreciating the Value of Social Proof

'Any fact is better established by two or three testimonies
than by a thousand arguments.'
Marie Dressler, actress

The term social proof was first introduced by Robert Cialdini in his 1984 book, *Influence* (Social Proof, 2022). Otherwise known as informational social influence, it is defined as a 'psychological phenomenon where people assume the actions of others reflect correct behaviour for a given situation'.

NLP could certainly be defined as ambiguous and therefore does lend itself to being one of those professions which could benefit from gathering more social proof on every level, especially if NLP were ever to become regulated at some point in the future.

Many NLP practitioners claim 'NLP works' and that this statement should be good enough to persuade people to part with their hard-earned cash. However, to believe NLP can become a successful and accepted profession simply based upon opinion, with no supporting evidence to back this up, is both arrogant and naive.

NLP Professionals, however, appreciate the value of having many different types of social proof to support their claims, because they understand potential clients may be looking at a variety of solutions to their particular issue and those clients need to evaluate and compare the options available.

NLP Professionals accept that operating in the real world means matching expectations of their potential clients and meeting them in their map of the world. They know social proof is a powerful way of pacing and leading a potential client and converting them into a paying client.

Personally, I think it's a good idea to have as much social proof as you can possibly get, because it all feeds in to the convincer strategies your potential clients may be using to assess your services. This is about meeting your clients in their model of the world. Your potential clients may value some or all of the following types of social proof – your remit, as an NLP Professional, is to ensure the social proof you receive is the sort your potential clients want to see.

Of course, it is also important to recognise that some forms of social proof may be more open to 'scams' and false claims. And most people who do use social proof as part of their decision making process will already have the skills to filter what is relevant to them – social media has empowered us all to be more discerning!

For NLP Professionals, credible forms of social proof can include:

- Personal testimonials and reviews
- Social media endorsement
- Narrative evidence
- External validation
- Third-party accreditation
- Professional memberships
- Research

Personal testimonials and reviews

The simplest and quickest way to start collecting social proof and evidence to add credibility to the services you offer is by asking for testimonials from your clients.

You can do this from the very first client you work with, or even with other students on your training course – after all, if you are able to help someone to resolve a challenge or guide them to make a significant transformational change, even in a training room environment or with a pro bono client, it's a starting point. Some newly certified NLP practitioners will work with clients in exchange for a testimonial rather than money, which is a win-win situation for both parties.

I remember when I started my coaching training, three of us set up a co-coaching group. This worked really well because there was always a coach, a client and an observer, who was able to comment on improvements. Not only were we practising and learning from each other, we also gave each other testimonials, which actually gave us all a boost of confidence as well as our first bit of social proof.

This works particularly well if you are delivering any pro bono coaching, either as part of your training or when you first start. Rather than offering something completely free, create some value for your services by asking for payment in the form of a testimonial.

Client reviews are also extremely powerful when it comes to encouraging potential clients to 'buy' your services. I could sell coals to Newcastle, as long as they are not my coals in the first place, so I relied on word of mouth and personal recommendations when I was running my accountancy business! I was incredibly lucky in that I never had to directly pitch for a piece of work, because my clients did it for me. Any satisfied client is a potential salesperson for your business, so make sure you capture their ringing endorsement of your services. Even if they would prefer to remain anonymous, they could still give you permission to use their initials and/or a vague job description: 'Joe Bloggs has empowered me to be a better manager and I would recommend their services to anyone wanting to improve their confidence' – A.B, Company Director.

Even if only one person takes notice of this testimonial/client review, it's one more client that has chosen you to be their NLP professional.

There is value in this type of third-party endorsement – after all, I wonder how often you may use product reviews on Amazon, TripAdvisor, Google and Which? to name a few. I know I will always check reviews when choosing between two similar products and I certainly look at online reviews for home and electrical products, even if I am actually buying the goods in a shop (rather than online). Reviews gathered in this way can be aninfluencer as well as having a direct impact on reputation. Reviews can greatly influence the potential success of restaurants and other venues.

As you start to collate your testimonials and reviews, you will find some of these naturally develop further into case studies, success stories and narrative evidence, which you can use to demonstrate the effect your services are having on your clients.

All you want to do is increase the odds of a potential client choosing you, so this is an easy win!

Social media endorsement

Twenty years ago, newspapers still sold in their millions and were underpinned by advertisers who paid huge sums of money. Advertising on websites was expensive and somewhat speculative – who was looking at the page? Were they the right person? The fact it was 'on the web' had a cachet and you paid the price to be an early adopter.

Now (2021), there are so many social media platforms it is a challenge to keep up – they have taken over as the easiest, most accessible and affordable place to network, especially because there are very few boundaries on social media.

Social proof in this arena has been ramped up accordingly, with social influencers being measured by the number of likes, followers, retweets and friends they can muster. People tend to follow a crowd and, like bees around a honey pot, will congregate where others are already hovering. I don't know about you, and I'm more likely to want to eat in a restaurant that's already busy and buzzing, because I assume that it is busy because the food is good! I know it is not always the right assumption to make...and it is a fact that people are naturally influenced by the actions of others – hence the phrase *social influencers*.

The main social media platforms that I am familiar with (Facebook, Twitter, LinkedIn Instagram, You Tube and TikTok) offer fantastic opportunities for promoting yourself, your business, your friends, colleagues and your events, without having to spend any money on advertising.

It would also be fair to say that social media has become inextricably linked with reputation – due to the general accessibility of information, the best way to get a response from a large organisation is to tweet them. Customer service via Twitter has become more effective because it is instant and visible, so customer issues are being played out in a public arena rather than being dealt with (or not) behind closed doors. My personal experience has been that Twitter has become rather good at being the platform for holding organisations to account, especially when it comes to customer service. Too often, when I have experienced a challenge with a company, I have been advised to take it up via Twitter rather than just send an email (which is ignored) or make a phone call (assuming you can even find a phone number).

It would be incongruent of me to pretend this is a trend I have embraced...apart from keeping resources up to date for ANLP's social media co-ordinator, I have abstained from social media for over three years now to give myself a break! As a former School Governor, I witnessed the challenges created by social media on occasions, which led to our school banning mobile phones, with positive results. Indeed, I'm thinking of doing the same at home, so when friends and family come to visit, we can talk together rather than watch them buried in their phones.

Despite this, I do recognise that social media, used well, has a huge part to play in building rapport with potential clients and raising profile, and is a great opportunity to shine a light and signpost the services on offer. I also know that one of the keys to using social media effectively is to be consistent…it is an immediate platform for engagement so if you are going to use it for gathering social proof, make sure you are updating your posts regularly. With the enormous amount of traffic flowing through all these platforms, posting once every couple of months is unlikely to build your social media endorsements.

I am still working on my own personal strategies and boundaries for using social media, so I can achieve a balance between engaging with others and not getting sucked into yet another cute cat video!

Narrative evidence

Narrative Evidence refers to anecdotal or personal evidence, such as that provided by interviews, exemplars, stories, testimonials and opinions (Tversky, 1973)

In her wonderful book, *Rising Strong* (Brown, 2015), Brené Brown prefaces her work with 'A Note on Research and Storytelling as Methodology'. She suggests that stories are a powerful format and can be considered relevant because 'the most useful knowledge about human behaviour is based upon people's lived experiences' (page xiii). As a research professor at the University of Houston, she certainly has some experience in this field.

I am in a really fortunate position, in that I do get to hear about other people's success with NLP on a regular basis. At the moment, some of these stories are shared in various ways, through *Rapport*, the ANLP and NLP Conference websites and of course, through the NLP Awards.

Every story I hear is about NLP making a difference to someone – I have heard stories about NLP Professionals helping after 9/11, air crashes, tsunamis and shootings. I have listened to Trainers telling me how much of a difference NLP has made in their lives and the lives of their students – the student who went on to take NLP into the prison service; the student who uses their NLP to make a difference in the justice system; the student who has revolutionised their teaching practice in their primary school.

What breaks my heart is that hardly any of these stories are recorded in any way, because these amazing professionals are 'just doing their job' or really don't see what a difference they are making in society. For them this is normal, this is what NLP does!

The NLP Awards, introduced in 2017, barely touch the surface of all the good that is being done out there. Past winners have included Francis Taylor, who uses his NLP to benefit the care system, based upon his own childhood experiences; Rita Aleluia, who plays a pivotal role in building awareness for NLP principles and processes by providing strategies for parents and teachers to become more self-aware, caring and effective educators of children; Dr Jeff Stoker, an NLP trained GP who has used his skills to integrate NLP into his own clinical practice to create positive changes and better results for his patients, as well as training his admin staff and colleagues in NLP techniques to help them engage with and communicate more effectively with patients; Ali Knowles who bridges the gap with young people using Olly and his superpowers to impart NLP skills to the younger generation; Fiona Stimson, who works at the Royal Marsden Hospital and uses NLP to support patients in extremely challenging times as they manage their journey with cancer ... these are just a very few examples of where NLP is quietly having a positive impact our society, day in, day out.

This will come as no surprise to us because we all know NLP works and it can make a huge difference to people's lives. We all have personal experience of this fact and I am sure we do all have many experiences we can relate and share. We can recall many occasions where NLP has made a positive difference to our lives and the lives of others...so please start capturing these stories and sharing them.

External validation

External validation is a stronger form of social endorsement because it demonstrates where recognised and respected organisations are utilising NLP as part of their services – with clients, staff and end users.

ANLP member Yvonne Fernando is currently heading up an NLP and Health project, exploring how NLP could support primary care and patients. They are building on Yvonne's experience of working with Charing Surgery, in Kent, to widen the support offered to a much larger number of GP practices and their patients. This is all possible because the project team includes GPs and others who work in primary healthcare, which means greater credibility from the outset, as the GPs within the team can talk with authority and credibility and offer narrative evidence to those for whom the project is being developed.

As soon as the pandemic struck in early 2020, ANLP Members Michael Dunlop, Lynn McKeown and Leanne McCafferty set up a COVID-19 specific digital resources NLP Project to support the Social Care workers in Northern Ireland (NISCC), providing manageable, accessible and sustainable support services to care staff when they absolutely needed it (Dunlop, 2020). The Social Care Council won 'Outstanding Team' at the European Social Services Awards for developing these resources to support the workforce.

ANLP Trainer member Emma McNally has done extensive work with Essex County Council, who developed CLICK, a hybrid training package shaped by Trauma Perceptive Practice and NLP (McNally, 2021). The council independently evaluated and evidenced the benefits and outcomes from the small-scale project and have scaled up. In an endorsement letter to ANLP, the Head of Strategic Commissioning and Policy at Essex County Council wrote: 'We would have no hesitation in endorsing NLP as a tool for self-development and professional practice, which in turn can play a role in supporting better outcomes for young people.'

Let's face it, these are pretty impressive pieces of external validation!

Third-party accreditation

In Chapter 3, I referred to the ambiguous language sometimes used by NLP Practitioners. It is quite possible the reason this ambiguous language can sometimes be used, is because it is understood one of the things both the public and industry frequently do look for is some sort of external validation for courses and Practitioners.

The public hear all sorts of negative stories in the press and as NLP is unregulated, they do seek some sort of reassurance that what they are about to invest in has been accredited, approved or recognised by a third party...and I am talking about a genuine, arms-length third party here, rather than another company or association which has been set up by the same person to imply third-party accreditation of their services, in other words a form of circular referencing (yes, this does happen).

It is a requirement for many areas of the public sector for workshops and courses to have external accreditation. I have, in the past, had conversations with NLP Professionals and representatives from the police force, the armed forces, schools and even HM Revenue and Customs. These NLP Professionals are requesting third-party verification for the courses they run, because this verification has been requested by their client. Representatives from the public sector are looking for courses which have been accredited or approved by an external body, as it is part of their internal policies to only run 'accredited courses' or hire in an 'approved professional'.

When you step into Perceptual Positions and look at this from the potential client's point of view, this is an understandable reaction. Quite often, the person responsible for hiring in the services of a professional has all sorts of checking procedures to complete, in order to demonstrate they have completed their due diligence and can justify why they have hired a particular practitioner to deliver training. Therefore, employing the services of a professional who does have some sort of external verification or accreditation for the courses they deliver can help with this process.

I know the depth of checks which sometimes have to be undertaken are rigorous, and rightly so. To be a school governor, even though it was a voluntary position, I had to undergo a Disclosure and Barring Service (DBS) check because I might come into contact with young people on occasions.

As a parent, I would certainly expect the school to run these external checks and validations on any person coming into contact with my child, because they have a legal obligation to me as a parent and they have a duty to ensure our children are safe when in their care.

Even individuals who don't have to comply with legal or moral obligations, often seek some sort of verification that the person they are about to choose does have approval or recognition from someone else.

For example, due to legislative changes, I had to purchase some new software for running the company accounts. It is quite important to report on the accounts correctly and meet all the criteria set out by HM Revenue and Customs.

Rather than just searching for 'accounts software' on the internet, the first thing I did was go onto the HM Revenue and Customs' website and find their list of 'HMRC approved software' because I knew this would have already been checked and I would be better off, in the long run, investing in something which had already been validated. It also saved me a lot of time on due diligence, because if HM Revenue and Customs had already checked and approved this software, then I could presume it works and it already meets their criteria.

So it is quite easy to understand why some individuals and companies do seek external validation for the services they are buying. It is their investment in terms of time, money and energy, so they do want some assurance their investment will be worth it, and by selecting something which has already been externally validated, they have completed some of their due diligence quickly and easily and have some justification for their choice.

If you have designed a piece of accounts software, it is quite easy to work out where to get it externally verified so you have a better chance of selling your product. This is because there is only one government agency responsible for ensuring accounts are correctly calculated, and that is HMRC. But where does a coach or NLP professional go to get such approval, validation or accreditation?

This does mean that for those options orientated NLP Professionals, there is more choice. For starters, it is your choice whether you want to get external validation for your work, just as the software developer can choose whether or not they get their accounts software approved.

If you do decide you want external verification for your services, workshops and courses, then there are different ways you can go about this.

Depending on the sector in which you deliver your courses, you may find there is sector specific accreditation you can achieve. For example, if you are developing or wanting to deliver courses that relate to leadership and management, you can get accreditation or approval from ILM, formerly known as the Institute for Leadership and Management, which now operates under the awarding organisation City and Guilds.

The alternative to sector specific approval is third-party accreditation from one of the bodies which oversees the field in which you practice, i.e. coaching or NLP.

For example, if you would like to use external accreditation, which underpins all your courses, you could have all your work as an NLP Trainer accredited by ANLP. Alternatively, you could opt to have your 'NLP for effective managers' course recognised by ILM and your 'Managing Autism using NLP' course recognised by the National Autistic Society (NAS).

ANLP do get regular enquiries from members of the public, wanting to check whether a particular trainer is accredited with ANLP, or a certain course is recognised by ANLP. When the answer is 'No, this course is not ANLP accredited', we are usually asked to provide details of an ANLP Accredited course or trainer.

So to those who question the value of external accreditation and debate whether there is a need for any accrediting body in NLP, I would say there is a definite need indicated in the level of enquiries we get from your potential clients.

Do you need your work to be accredited by anyone else? My answer would be to ask what your potential clients are looking for in the way of credibility and reassurance and deliver what your clients are seeking. ANLP Accredited Trainer, Luke Bong, wrote a powerful *Rapport* article entitled 'The Value of Accreditation', which documents his journey and the benefits he experienced as a result (Bong, 2018).

There is a demand for external accreditation, both from NLP Trainers and from their potential clients (especially in the public sector, health and education sectors). So if NLP Professionals wish to have their work independently checked and externally validated, it is right that they have options through which they can achieve third-party accreditation.

For those who don't believe in it or feel they don't need it, then it is OK – it is a choice. I do believe NLP Professionals, who understand the importance of social proof and external verification, are more likely to have their work independently accredited and value the intangible benefits of accreditation.

Professional memberships

It would be a little remiss of me to be CEO of the Association for NLP and then not mention Professional Memberships in a book for NLP Professionals.

Seriously, one of the ways to demonstrate social proof is to belong to the Trade Associations or Professional Membership bodies relating to your area of expertise, whether this is NLP, Coaching, Hypnotherapy or Thought Field Therapy.

Professional Membership bodies provide practitioners with a form of self-regulation and accountability for their profession, and most credible professions do have at least one Professional Body.

I would take a marketer who belongs to the Chartered Institute of Marketing (CIM) more seriously than a marketer who doesn't belong to any professional or trade association. When we were building our house, I always looked for trades who belonged to some professional association for extra reassurance. In fact, I used to check their membership association had a complaints process, so there was some form of redress should anything go wrong – I discovered the hard way that it is a good idea to have every extra piece of reassurance possible.

I know from calls we receive in the ANLP office, your potential clients are thinking the same thing, and seeking the extra reassurance which comes from belonging to a Trade Association. For every person who calls the office enquiring about locating a practitioner in their area, we must get at least one call enquiring about whether a particular training company is registered with us. So, the indications are your potential clients also give credence to whether or not you belong to your Professional Body or Trade Association.

As I mentioned earlier, professional bodies fall under a similar remit to third-party accreditation and indeed, many members of Professional bodies use this as their informal 'accreditation'. Again, do be aware of companies masquerading as professional bodies who may not be as independent or 'arms length' as they seem.

Research

When the ASA remit was expanded, social proof requirements were taken to a whole new level – supporting evidence for claims within the health environment have now taken on a whole new meaning and NLP, like many other helping professions, has to move forward with obtaining clinical evidence to prove its claims.

Realistically, the NLP profession cannot produce the body of evidence required by the ASA overnight – their requirements are rigorous, detailed and are necessary for each of the medical conditions in which NLP can be used with good effect. These conditions include 'feeling down or feeling blue', aches and pains, confidence, fears and phobias, stress, guilt and smoking cessation.

Clinical research of this type is essential if we are to ever have NLP acknowledged as a viable helping profession within therapeutic and clinical settings. NLP research, even the type that is not necessarily recognised as robust enough by the ASA, plays a valuable role in raising awareness and adding to the credibility of NLP.

Scepticism does exist, especially in the health, education and some organisational sectors, and this scepticism can be managed differently, depending on the context (see Chapter 8).

When considering the health sector in particular, practitioners frequently require evidence something works. Whilst the average man in the street or small business has the autonomy to make their own decisions, many larger organisations, education authorities and Clinical Commissioning Groups (CCGs) have to be able to justify their proposed investment in an NLP practitioner because they are publicly funded and we, the taxpayers, expect them to spend these funds wisely.

We would be appalled if the FDA or Medicines and Healthcare Products Regulatory Agency were to approve a new drug for general release without ensuring it had been rigorously tested first, and there was evidence to ensure every aspect of the new drug's performance had been checked and passed as safe.

Testimonials, success stories and case studies do give subjective accounts of how NLP has worked for a particular individual or with a particular issue, and these, in themselves, are not likely to be enough to sway a regulatory board of NHS professionals, who are making decisions about how best to allocate their health budget for the coming year.

We trust our GP to recommend only what is safe and what will work, and you can imagine what could happen if they were to prescribe a drug purely on the basis their mother-in-law's neighbour's cousin had tried it and reported it was 'quite good'.

There are ways of challenging, testing and recording what we do, regardless of the fact there is a lot of subjectivity involved. Clinical research can be dismissed both within and outside the NLP community for this reason.

Quite often, NLP practitioners will argue that because NLP is so subjective, it cannot be formally and robustly researched in any way, as NLP methods cannot be measured in clinically or academically robust ways. I am sure I remember learning in NLP 'cannot' is simply another choice – we 'can' choose to 'not' do something?

The whole reason for the International NLP Research Conferences (2008–2012) were to initiate some valid enquiries into NLP and start to find a body of evidence to support and evidence the claims 'NLP works'.

Since then, there have been and continue to be a number of well-researched and documented papers that have been published in a variety of academic journals. The NLPWiki website (NLP Information and Research, 2022) has valuable resources detailing the references and abstracts for positive, direct and indirect published research for NLP and provides a more balanced perspective than Wikipedia.

Current Research in NLP Volumes 1–3 (2009–2013), are peer-reviewed academic journals published following the Research Conferences, which contain academically robust and rigorous papers about the applications of NLP in various settings, specifically education, psychology and business.

There are NLP research projects continuing all over the UK and abroad:

- With the support of Richard Churches, Lead Advisor – Research and Evidence Based Practice, The Education Development Trust publishes research specific to the education sector and has supported and published powerful NLP related research. This research helps teachers and educational establishments make favourable decisions regarding the inclusion of NLP in their training programmes. Two of Richard's research papers, plus others are available to download from the ANLP website (NLP Research Papers, 2019).

- Frank Bourke and Rick Gray have been driving forward the Research and Recognition project (Research and Recognition Project Home Page, 2022) in the USA for many years, which is focused on PTSD and has developed the Reconsolidation of Traumatic Memories (RTM) protocols for using with the treatment of PTSD. This work continues in the UK, with Dr Lisa de Rijk leading a team of researchers, who are undertaking an initial Randomised Control Trail (RCT), which compares the RTM protocol with Trauma Focussed CBT (Dr de Rijk, 2021).

- Dr Phil Parker has been very successful in getting his NLP and Lightning Process research published in academic journals, including *Fatigue: Biomedicine, Health and Behaviour* (Dr Parker, 2021). His work focuses on chronic health conditions like Myalgic Encephalomyelitis (ME) also known as Chronic Fatigue Syndrome (CFS).

It is important to understand that, to be taken seriously, we do need to have enough confidence in our own area of expertise (NLP) to challenge the claims we make, by being seen to question and challenge aspects of NLP, and by evidencing, disproving and validating the work we do.. Of course the research aspect of NLP vitally important for raising the credibility of using NLP for therapeutic interventions with the wider public.

Summary

Social proof is important for any emerging field, especially those, like NLP, which have some ambiguity around them. Social proof can include research, independent accreditation, testimonials and membership of professional bodies.

So how does all this potential social proof benefit you as a Professional and NLP as a field?

I believe there is a case for collating a body of evidence and social proof to prove it the effectiveness of NLP. Without this, as legislation and regulation increases, NLP will be shelved in favour of other, more evidence-based approaches which can offer proof to support their claims.

Actions

- Collect testimonials from your next three clients and use them on your website and in your promotional materials (NB Make sure they comply with CAP guidelines).
- Join a Professional Body or Trade Association. It would be great if this was ANLP...and any professional membership will add to your social proof.

CHAPTER 5
Celebrating the Diversity of NLP

'For too long, we have focused on our differences – in our politics and backgrounds, in our race and beliefs – rather than cherishing the unity and pride that binds us together.'

Bob Riley, American politician

NLP is a hugely diverse field of practice and sometimes, some practitioners of NLP can get bogged down in the differences between themselves and their competitors, believing that they have to find a way of disempowering or discrediting their competitors in order to attract more clients.

NLP Professionals like you understand the bigger picture and are able to chunk up...and chunk down again. You are able to celebrate the differences between you and your perceived competitors, realising it is all about respecting other models of the world and accepting there are different training models for NLP – which all have a part to play in the developing field of NLP. The thing we all have in common is...NLP.

Diversity is healthy and allows you to stand out in your chosen profession. Being different to your fellow practitioners of NLP is one of the most powerful marketing tools you have and will make you stand out as an NLP Professional.

In order to recognise the value of NLP as a profession and accept we all have a part to play in delivering NLP to the public, let's take an open minded look at the NLP community to which we all belong.

Chunking up...

Over the years, the NLP Community has diversified in many different ways, resulting in a number of certifying bodies, whose trainers deliver NLP in a number of different ways, which have evolved and adapted to meet the needs of the public.

I think all types of courses have their place within the NLP community because it very much depends on the potential student's reasons for wanting to learn more about NLP. All can bring great value to the public and play a part in creating a positive impact within society.

One of the presuppositions of NLP is all about respecting another person's model of the world – so couldn't this diversity mean that we have found more than one way of delivering NLP? That this just emphasises our flexibility?

Put yourself in the shoes of a potential client for a moment. Imagine you are looking for a NLP practitioner to help you with a particular challenge you are facing (content isn't important here).

What are you looking for in this practitioner? As a member of the public, with all due respect to certification bodies, are you really interested in whether they have qualified through the International NLP Trainers Association (INLPTA) or the Society of NLP (SNLP) or the International Training Association (ITA) or the American Board of NLP (ABNLP) or online via Udemy or one of the other online training establishments that pops up weekly.

In fact, do you, as a potential client, understand anything about the different lineages and practitioner certificates never mind know the difference between INLPTA, SNLP, ITA ABNLP and Udemy?

What other things would a potential client take into consideration when evaluating your services? Could there be other things which concern you more than where your practitioner obtained their certification?

I choose my GP based on many criteria, including recommendation, reputation, location and possibly even their appearance, and I have never chosen my GP based upon which educational establishment they attended.

As a member of the NLP community, *you* may be interested in where your colleagues trained – and what interests you within the NLP community is completely different to what interests a potential client.

It may be true that within the GP community, the information about their original educational establishment is significant, and I am sure there is qualification snobbery in their profession, just as there is with universities and NLP...and as time goes on, our experience and our ability to apply our learnings (as a GP, a graduate or an NLP practitioner) takes on more significance than where we trained.

TIP

Think about what your potential clients really want to know about you – they may be more interested in how you can help them solve their problem.

Remember one of the chunking up exercises you may have done whilst you were on your NLP training. I recall sitting with a partner, and being asked to say something factual about myself and what I did. When I finished speaking, my partner simply responded with something like, 'That's great. And you are so much more than that. What else are you?'

In a few short moments I went from being 'just an accountant' to being someone really superb, wonderful and awesome (for me, at least). This was a valuable lesson in chunking up, and it does apply to us all – we are all so much more than the number of hours we trained or the NLP lineage we followed. It is this diversity that we can utilise when differentiating our services.

If we were to chunk up to find our shared perspective, it's quite easy to spot that one of them is, we all share a common interest – NLP!

When it comes to NLP, we are lucky, because we already all share some positive beliefs about the power of NLP, the difference it can make and the fact it works. This, in itself, is immensely empowering for us as individuals, for our colleagues and for the whole field of NLP. Imagine what could happen if we were to take those positive beliefs which reside within the community and really use them to celebrate our successes, which all come from some shared positive beliefs that NLP can make a difference to others.

So doesn't this discussion revolve more about elevating the field of NLP to such an extent so that we have the whole gamut of experience, expertise and narrative evidence (aka case studies and stories) to draw upon?

...Chunking down

We are so lucky to have experience of a subject which is hugely diverse in its applications, because it means we can all find slightly different ways of applying our skills, which means overall there will be more people able to benefit from NLP.

I remember inwardly debating with myself which subject to take at university. If I had chosen biology, I had a vast choice of potential universities I could attend, because virtually every university in the UK offered a degree in biology. But what I really wanted to do was genetics, because this was the subject which really fascinated me. At the time, my choice of UK universities was limited to only six (I'm showing my age now, as I'm sure there is a lot more choice for potential geneticists nowadays). But because there were only six universities which offered genetics as a subject, you can be assured every budding geneticist immediately focused on those six universities and completely ignored the rest.

Like genetics, NLP is a specialised subject in itself, and has such a vast range of potential applications, the opportunities are virtually limitless. There are NLP practitioners who specialise in using NLP for weight loss, for increasing confidence, for team building, for dyslexia, for relationships, for phobias, for managing ill health, for allergies, for improving communication skills, for enhancing performance and even for improving eyesight...and I am sure you can think of many others.

You are unique in recognising and understanding the practical applications of NLP when combined with your life experiences and skills in a certain way. It therefore follows you are best placed to apply your NLP skills in those areas you already understand and niche your services accordingly.

I met a teacher on an NLP training course and her passion was getting NLP into education. As a head teacher, she was very well placed to introduce NLP from the inside.

She had successfully done this in her own school, and because she had such recognisable success, she had been headhunted by the local authority and asked to do the same in a failing school within the same area. She applied the models which worked, and when I met her, she was starting to achieve some small steps towards success with the new school, and was working on a project to roll this out to other schools in her area.

There are many NLP Trainers I know who have successfully combined their NLP skills with their existing experience and created something unique in their field.

Recently retired NLP Trainer Julie Inglis successfully combined her personal experiences with her NLP skills and delivered courses in Hertfordshire for 'Managing Autistic Spectrum Conditions and ADHD using NLP'.

Both Hertfordshire County Council and the local Developing Special Needs Locally group (DSPL) subsidised these courses, because they had the evidence to prove their key workers have a greater impact with the people in their care once they have some relevant NLP skills to include in their portfolio. They measured this impact from a financial perspective and had proof the council saved money on adult care because they were using NLP.

This meant that in Hertfordshire at least, parents, carers, social workers and other key staff had the opportunity to learn about NLP and how it can make a difference to their lives and the lives of those affected by Asperger's, autism and ADHD.

Julie was driven by a passion which came from personal understanding because her children are on the autistic spectrum. I have attended this course and I know what a difference it makes because my younger son is also on the spectrum. Thanks to the foresight of Hertfordshire County Council, there are now people throughout Hertfordshire who are also experiencing the difference NLP can make to their lives.

TIP

By applying your NLP to areas you already understand and niching your services, you automatically create some credibility within your targeted field. As one of my mentors, Bev James would say, 'generalists seek clients and clients seek specialists'.

Richard Churches, who I mentioned earlier, is the Lead Advisor – Research and Evidence Based Practice, for The Education Development Trust. Richard has been an Advanced Skills Teacher, as well as a manager in inner city secondary schools in London and an Ofsted Inspector. He has been a senior leader and advisor in many government-led education initiatives. He is therefore well placed and experienced in the education field.

Richard combines this experience with his understanding of NLP and has been responsible for some very interesting and enlightening books and research papers, including *NLP for Teachers*, which he co-authored with Roger Terry (Churches, 2007). He has been able to secure research funding for NLP in education and continues to work within the education sector to introduce the concepts of NLP into the education system.

Contrast this with a call I received a few years ago now, from a concerned dad. His 18-year-old daughter had recently been on a transformational weekend, and as a result, now wanted to leave university (where she had been for less than a term) and pursue her career as an NLP practitioner. She had been promised a fantastic deal whereby she would become an NLP Trainer within three months and be earning vast amounts of money within a year.

This dad was, quite rightly, a little sceptical and concerned about his daughter's intentions to become an NLP Trainer earning a six-figure salary in just one year. I asked what she was studying at university, that she was so keen to give up and It turned out she was studying drama and acting. Clearly, this dad wanted the best for his daughter and was looking for some guidance from ANLP, having come up against an unscrupulous trainer who was behaving in a far from professional way (I hasten to add the trainer concerned was not a member of ANLP). By talking things through with this dad, and offering him some different perspectives, he was able to find an acceptable compromise to propose to his daughter.

The suggestion was that rather than drop out of University altogether, his daughter could continue her university studies alongside studying NLP, because once she graduated, it could be quite possible for her to create a niche of clients within the acting profession who would benefit from her skills.

By combining your skills with what you already know and understand, as well as raising your credibility as an NLP Professional within your own field of expertise, you are also creating a solid foundation for your NLP business. Your target audience could be right there in front of you. After all, if you have benefitted from applying NLP in your life, so could your work colleagues, associates and clients.

ANLP Member Dr Suzanne Henwood did just this, and once she had completed her NLP training, she started introducing NLP into the health sector. As a clinical radiographer and academic, she was able to do this because she could translate her NLP into terms which were more acceptable to a healthcare professional and bridge the language gap between the health service and NLP.

In fact, after my surgery, I did give my surgeon a copy of her book, *NLP and Coaching for Healthcare Professionals* (Henwood, 2007), because I realised this was more likely to resonate with him and maybe strike a greater chord of understanding than some of the other great NLP books I know and love.

TIP

NLP Professionals provide solutions – ask yourself what your niche could be and what problems would your niche solve?

Once you have a clear idea about what area you could develop as your specific niche, you will find it much easier to create your marketing plan and identify your target market of clients. Then you will be able to devise your promotional and marketing materials so you are able to build rapport and communicate with your potential clients really effectively.

I do understand it is tempting to want to keep your options open rather than limit your stream of potential clients, so I would encourage you to think for a moment: when you need someone to fix the damage to your expensive Victorian oak flooring, you are likely to search for an oak flooring specialist, rather than a straightforward carpenter. Your Victorian oak flooring is valuable to you and you would prefer to hire a specialist to repair your damaged floor.

The same applies to NLP – it is quite a challenging subject to sell in the first place, so if you are promoting yourself as being able to fix all things to all people, how are your potential clients going to specifically understand how you can help them? Presumably, you would rather stand out in your particular area of expertise and attract those clients who really will benefit from your help.

I certainly messed up when I went charging full pelt into my new coaching business, joining the breakfast networking group without even making any real plans first. What type of coaching did I want to do? Who were my intended clients? Where would I be most likely to find these clients?

Once I stepped back and thought about my actions, and my longer term plans, I realised I was never likely to find my clients at a breakfast business networking group, because my dream was to join with other NLP practitioners so we could collectively make a bigger difference. I wasn't likely to find too many of them networking in the golf club at 7 a.m. every week.

What had happened to me in this situation was I had become very motivated whilst in the safe environment of the coaching weekend, which had really opened my eyes to the wealth of new possibilities. I was a bit like the child in the sweetie shop, wanting some of everything...now... without considering the consequences and the alternative ways of getting to sample all the sweets in the shop.

I realised then how important it is that we have a clear outcome and plan for what we do want to achieve, so we do have something to focus on and keep us on the right track, especially when we do get out into the real world.

TIP

To help you identify your niche, identify those people you enjoy working with most – could they become your niche market? Where have you used your NLP skills to create big changes in your own life or others...maybe that is your niche?

It is the differences in our approach, in our application and in the way we have been taught which contribute so much to the continual evolution of NLP. We are privileged to be involved with a relatively new subject and its flexibility means we are always refining, improving and discovering new ways of applying the things we have learned and understood from our own NLP training.

NLP itself was derived from modelling various therapies and approaches, and NLP has continued to evolve and contribute to other related subjects such as Clean Language and New Code NLP.

These differences are healthy and contribute to the continual evolution of products and services from which we can all benefit.

Take Mr Dyson, for example. Vacuum cleaners had already been around for a very long time – in one form or another our mothers and grandmothers had used them, and over the years, they had evolved (and diversified) into either a cylinder or upright model. These types of vacuum cleaners had been around for many decades and apart from some cosmetic enhancements, had changed very little. We all accepted and used these machines and probably thought no more about it.

Then Dyson came along and completely revolutionised the world of the vacuum cleaner – he managed to find even better ways of cleaning which were completely different to anything which had gone before. He developed a whole new range of products using his revolutionary new technology and transformed the world of vacuum cleaners…simply by being a bit different.

NLP is a wonderful subject for keeping us on our toes and offers us the opportunity to be creative and develop further applications and uses. As another challenge arises in our world, it is fairly certain someone will work out how NLP can be applied to this challenge.

I see NLP as a bit like giving a child a cardboard box. If you watch a child playing with a cardboard box, their natural curiosity and imagination knows no boundaries. When we moved house, my son created a whole new world of possibilities. The packing boxes were transformed into robots and houses and spaceships and trucks and beds. They were chopped up and stuck together and coloured and decorated…they provided hours of endless fun and creativity and imagination and possibilities in the mind of a young child.

Isn't this exactly what NLP gives us – opportunities, possibilities and the chance to be creative and discover new resources? It is this curiosity and creativity and different ways of thinking which contribute to the development of NLP. One person looks at the cardboard box and sees a spaceship…and another sees a submarine or a robot. All are right because NLP, like a cardboard box, has at least 101 potential uses.

TIP

Explaining what you do is much easier when you have a niche. Try completing the sentence, 'I help/support people to…'

As I mentioned, one of the models we sometimes seem to adopt in the NLP community is division. There are some infamous splits within the NLP community, the most widely recognised being Richard Bandler and John Grinder, two of the co-founders of NLP.

I believe it is time to acknowledge these divisions, recognise the benefits…and move on.

It is common knowledge Bandler and Grinder publicly disagreed and fell out over NLP. This is OK, whatever happened is between Richard and John, and none of us, as observers, will ever know everything that really went on…as long as we remember 'the map is not the territory' and apply this to their situation as well.

We do know despite their later differences, they co-created something which we all find useful and beneficial. They created it, and collectively, ever since they shared their ideas back in the 1970s, we have all played a part in the continued development and evolution of NLP.

Bandler and Grinder have gone their separate ways, and they have each developed new ideas based on NLP for themselves. Others have come together since then, developed ideas and publicly split as well. It seems some of the early movers and shakers in NLP have inadvertently created models which often divide the community.

I must admit, I do wonder sometimes, how this could have happened, given the presuppositions of NLP – principles which form the foundation of NLP and have been modelled from key people who consistently produce superb results, as well as from systems theory and natural laws.

We are taught these are useful beliefs to adopt and can help us to make some sense of the world. In which case, perhaps we do need to assume at the time, these divisions occurred because behind every behaviour is a positive intention. The one presupposition which could usefully be applied now is 'having respect for another person's model of the world'.

Some of those early co-creators of NLP may choose to never speak to each other again – the point is, does it really affect us? NLP has and continues to evolve since then, because we all play a part in influencing how NLP moves forward from now on.

We can choose to decide division within the community may have a positive intention for the few people who follow this model (they seem to have many impassioned followers), and it does have a detrimental effect on NLP as a whole and can cause massive confusion for the public…who then walk away and try something else instead, because they have no idea who they should train with and what lineage is best.

Of course, we will forever be extremely grateful to John, Richard and the originators of NLP for what they co-created. Now, NLP Professionals are choosing to model the best parts of NLP, and leaving behind the divisions between lineages. There is great value in respecting each other's model of the world and acknowledging that all these lineages had a part to play in the evolution of NLP. As a professional field, this enables us to move towards a more united NLP community which accepts the differences within it, celebrates the successes and similarities and starts to focus outwards towards the society in which we want to make a difference.

Summary

By chunking up and recognising all NLP Professionals have some-thing to offer to the NLP Profession, you will recognise the diversity in NLP is about niching your services. By niching your services and becoming an expert in your particular NLP area of expertise, you will attract those clients seeking a specialist to help them address a particular issue. Overall, you will be contributing to NLP becoming more widely recognised as a credible solution for helping with lots of specific issues.

Actions

Identify your niche market, by asking yourself the following questions:

- What is your potential niche?
- What problems could your potential niche possibly solve?
- Why do these problems continue?
- Who do you most enjoy working with?

CHAPTER 6
Working Collaboratively

'The whole is more than the sum of its parts.'
Aristotle, philosopher

Many NLP practitioners currently run 'small businesses', when using the UK definition of a small company.* They stand proudly and independently, and sometimes view any form of collaboration with a fellow NLP practitioner as 'fraternising with the enemy'.

As an NLP Professional you realise the power of working collaboratively and pooling resources on occasions, so collectively we can get NLP out there into the public arena and make sure we are noticed.

NLP Professionals can recognise the 'power of the people', especially when it comes to working towards recognition of NLP as an accepted profession and with regard to any potential regulation or legislation.

I'd like to sow a few seeds and suggest some reframes which could make a difference to the way you view your business, and perhaps even NLP as a whole.

Think for a moment, of Aristotle's famous quote. He made this observation a few thousand years ago, and maybe it still holds true today? The whole concept of collaboration and fellowship is to maintain your own identity whilst working with others.

NLP is still an evolving profession compared to most other professions, so is still relatively unknown compared to some other, more established practices, such as CBT. We are getting wider recognition now and when I was recently talking with NLP Trainer, Fiona Campbell, she said "It feels like NLP is on the cusp, after all these years. It is an exciting time for us."

That said, there is still plenty of work to be done in getting NLP noticed out there.

Remember your basic chemistry lessons from school days. Even though I have a scientific background, I am still fascinated by the miracles of nature. So whilst this is very simplistic, it illustrates the point:

At a young age, when I was first introduced to the wonderful world of chemical reactions, I remember being absolutely fascinated by the equation

$$2H + O \longrightarrow H_2O$$

You will remember this means when hydrogen and oxygen are combined, they make water. Isn't this an amazing act of nature (or science) which can take two gases, and effectively combine them to create water, an essential part of our lives without which none of us could survive. On their own, neither hydrogen nor oxygen can even be seen, yet when they team up together, they create something completely different and certainly something bigger and more noticeable than either of them when taken in isolation.

There are many examples of successful partnerships outside the chemical world. I know I am showing my age, but do you recall Morecambe and Wise, the comedy duo who combined their skills, timing and talent to become one of the most famous and successful comedy acts ever in the UK? In fact, even if you are younger than me, you will probably have come across them because their Christmas specials are still repeated year after year and feature in every 'best of' programme ever made.

I'm not for one moment suggesting you go out tomorrow and look for an NLP partner with whom you can join forces and become the biggest double act since Morecambe and Wise. I am, for now, inviting you to chunk up around the whole concept of the 'whole being greater than the sum of its parts', and start to think about NLP being the 'whole'. Then we will become the parts which could combine to create something bigger and more noticeable like the NLP Profession.

This is the concept behind my Daffodil Principle, which is modelled on Wordsworth's poem, *I wandered lonely as a cloud*:

Imagine, for a moment, a daffodil. One daffodil is unique, individual and beautiful when captured in solitude, where its beauty can be focused upon and magnified; notice the colour combinations and perfect tonality between the trumpet of the daffodil and its petals; notice how it stands in magnificent splendour, tall, upright and proud.

Now think about a whole field containing 10,000 daffodils, all standing tall and proud, their brilliant yellow petals catching the spring sunshine, and a ripple of movement as the slight breeze catches them. Collectively they form a sea of bright yellow which seems to stretch as far as the eye can see – and for a moment, the impact of this magnificent yellow ocean completely takes your breath away.

To get NLP noticed and making an impact in society, we do need to combine our individual strengths always, and pull together our unique talents so NLP creates the same impact as the host of golden daffodils, which inspired Wordsworth.

This works well for daffodils, but does it work with people?

NLP was originally modelled on individuals rather than teams or groups, so I think there is a tendency, on occasions, for us to believe we can do it on our own. Sometimes, however omnipotent we would like to think we are, there is great value in working together to get NLP noticed, so we can collectively start to make a bigger difference.

A perfect example of this is those big charity events, such as Children in Need or Comic Relief, which now take place regularly and raise millions of pounds. People from all over the UK pull together and combine their resources to make these events happen.

Celebrities set an example (and use their celebrity status) to pull in the money for these worthy causes and engage with us all, encouraging us all to do our bit…and we see the results of this as the totals raised get bigger every year. It is fun, it is enjoyable, and we get a sense of team spirit and satisfaction from being part of something bigger and playing a small part in contributing to the monies raised which really will make a difference to many people.

How could we apply this to NLP? It may be obvious and yet it is very relevant to suggest that, as a field still working towards professionalism, it's important that we work together to combine our resources, share our skills and our successes and do our bit to ensure *NLP* gets out there and is noticed?

If you need reminding about the potential benefits of collaboration, think, for a moment, of a rainbow. The sun and rain, when they do combine their resources, create a magnificent array of colours in a rainbow…which most people do tend to notice. You may see collaborations elsewhere and I notice the magnificence of nature at every turn.

Closer to home, the NLP International Conference is a really great example of collaboration on every level. When ANLP were given the opportunity to take over the running of the conference in 2016, I felt slightly daunted by the prospect, despite having a clear belief that the conference was a really important community resource. People in the NLP Community volunteered their services and joined the conference team, to assist with getting the conference relaunched in 2017. I do think team collaboration and understanding of the bigger picture impact carried the team through and gave them the driving force to ensure success. The team were motivated by each other along the way and did all have a sense or what we they were creating would be significant and positively beneficial for NLP as a whole.

As the conference continues to evolve, especially with the advent of the virtual conference in 2021, so do the collaborations that are sparked at the conference. Indeed, Emma McNally and Lynn Robinson developed a new collaborative business spanning two continents, simply by meeting during Robert Dilts and Ian McDermott's masterclass at the conference in 2018.

The concept of sharing and collaboration is a challenging model to adopt sometimes, especially in the field of NLP, where more divisive models have been used in the past. This is changing and I believe the future of NLP lies in encouraging a more collaborative approach.

A couple of years ago I read Robert B Dilts' *Success Factor Modeling* (Vol 1) (Dilts, 2015) and it really gave me greater clarity about the role ANLP plays and the role I personally play in striving towards a greater vision. Dilts refers to 'Creating a world to which people want to belong' and whilst I had always understood ANLP has a role to play, I wasn't always crystal clear about how and where we fitted in the field of NLP.

As I mentioned right at the beginning of the book, I have a dream for NLP to be more widely recognised so it is embraced by society as a solution to many of life's challenges. I'm pretty confident that this is actually the vision for the field of NLP, rather than just being my dream.

So what part does ANLP play in achieving this vision – what is ANLP's mission? That's easy – ANLP's mission is to be the *Global Flagbearers for Professional NLP*...which is a bit of a relief really, given the title of this book.

The point is we do all have a part to play in achieving this vision for the field of NLP; we sit alongside those who want to set standards, run trainings, offer coaching and we will achieve this vision far more effectively when we collaborate and work together towards this common goal – let's get this amazing field of daffodils noticed.

I was fortunate enough to attend 'Passion in Action' a few years ago, an NLP workshop specifically run to support social enterprises and community projects. I was listening to Judith DeLozier and

Judith Lowe explain the concept of sharing. It was important and significant for us all to understand, at the time, that sharing ideas was a good thing to do and was different to sharing money. Their simple explanation went as follows:

> If I give you a pound and you give me a pound, then we each walk away with a pound. If I share my idea with you and you share your idea with me, then we each walk away with two ideas…which could then become three or more, as we use those ideas to generate others.

Remember, someone else understanding or knowing about NLP does not affect your understanding and knowledge of NLP! Surgeons, like Atul Gawande, frequently share their skills, knowledge and discoveries about new and better operating techniques, so the whole of medicine, and therefore the patients, benefit from these enhancements. Gawande modelled Boeing's pre flight checklists to develop a very basic surgical safety checklist – effectively, a pre flight checklist for surgeons. This checklist has been adopted by the World Health Organisation to improve the safety of surgical care around the world. Thank goodness he was willing to share his work.

In the same way, all those people who contribute to the NLP international conference are happy to share their expertise with others, so this information can be more widely understood and appreciated. The COVID-19 resources on the ANLP website, which have now been repurposed to Bitesize Video Resources (Bitesize Video Resources, 2020), are a valuable resource for anyone wanting to access quick bitesize pieces of NLP and they were provided by members of ANLP. We have all experienced this momentum, the surge of energy which comes from being part of a group of like-minded people. We know there is power in numbers, because we have probably all witnessed situations where the energy of a group takes us forward and possibly gives us enough confidence to do something we would not necessarily have done if we were on our own. The Tony Robbins firewalk springs to mind and is modelled by many others – it perfectly models collaboration and teamwork in order to create greater confidence and motivation in the individuals within the team.

TIP

Join the weekly ANLP Community Café or monthly Trainers meeting or quarterly Facebook Live so you can share space with like-minded people. Join a 'local' Practice Group because now most of them run virtually, it's so much easier to get involved…and if there isn't one locally, then collaborate with other local NLP professionals and set one up.

Like Emma and Lynn, referred to earlier, I do know of other NLP Professionals who form collaborative partnerships and associate groups with their colleagues because this does create a sense of confidence for potential clients – the perception there is something bigger rather than just one person does seem to make a difference to a client, even if they only deal with you.

If I can digress into the retail world for a moment, think about Bicester Village. It is probably one of the most well-known Outlet Retail Parks in the UK, and people travel from all over the UK to visit it. Yet Bicester Village is simply a very successful combination of small shops which have combined their designer names and individual reputations to create a centre that attracts millions of visitors every year (and who all seem to visit the same day I choose to go).

Very few people had heard of the little town of Bicester before Bicester Village opened, and I do know of the incredible impact this collaborative venture has had, because it is the area in which I grew up.

For most NLP professionals, there is a great benefit to creating a network of contacts, especially because many of us do work in isolation. Not only is there a benefit from sharing time and resources with colleagues, there is also the opportunity to create a contact list of other NLP professionals in the local area. Imagine how useful this could be the next time you may need a bit of extra help with your business.

Eve Menezes Cunningham, a journalist for *Rapport* magazine, wrote a wonderful article about 'how being extra helpful can be good for business' (Menezes-Cunningham, 2009). She explained how valuable it could be to help out a potential client by referring them on to someone else if there is some reason you cannot help them at this time, rather than just saying 'no'. Some people tend to remember acts of kindness and those times when someone has gone the extra mile, and it can reap benefits in the long run.

I do remember a few years ago, being so busy with my accounts work I recommended a potential client to another accountant, as I felt I could not give them the service they deserved at the time. Later the same year, when I was not quite so busy, the same accountant recommended me to a potential client, who turned out to be a hugely enjoyable and lucrative client to work with.

I have witnessed many positive collaborations, including one NLP Trainer and psychotherapist, who has a great network of contacts which he has created. As a psychotherapist, he has a brilliant arrangement with some of his business contacts whereby they cross-refer, so he takes on those clients who require a more psychotherapeutic approach. His business colleagues take on some of those clients who require a more straightforward NLP/coaching model.

So having a network of contacts can reap rewards, even if they are in the same field in which you already work.

TIP

Get together with local NLP Professionals and consider working together to promote your services. It is better to run one combined workshop than cancel two smaller ones because the numbers were not sufficient.

At this point, I would like to reiterate the difference between rivalry and competition:

> 'Competition', as defined by the Collins dictionary, is 'a contest in which a winner is selected from among two or more entrants'.
> A 'rival', as defined by the same dictionary, is 'a person or thing that is considered the equal of another'.

So, if we were to compete with each other for business, there is an inference that there will be winners and losers, and in a way this is true – only one person can win a particular piece of work.

So let's reframe for a moment and imagine what could happen if our attitude was more about having rivals than having competition. We could then enjoy a healthy rivalry with our colleagues in the field of NLP, rather than feeling the need to compete with them at every level and be the winner.

Think of sport, for example, where week in, week out, on various pitches, fields, arenas and tracks around the world, sports rivals compete to be the best in their chosen sport. There are clear winners, and losers, and the rivalry is fierce both between the competitors and between their rival supporters. But despite this rivalry and competition on the field, there is usually a healthy respect between players and athletes, both on and off the field. Tennis players, who may be competing in the same high-level competition, also practice together on the training courts before those big matches. Rival football stars from different premier league teams come together for the sake of a charity match…it does happen!

Contrast this approach with the one taken by politicians during an election. During an election campaign, in any one constituency, political hopefuls are competing against their opposition to win a seat and represent their party in parliament. Their primary objective is to win the seat so their party becomes the one to lead the country.

However, there seems to be no love lost between candidates, and in our constituency, they seem to spend more of their time telling us how bad their opposition is, rather than informing us about how good they will be in the role of MP. It appears that if they can use words to effectively denigrate and destroy their opposition, they will do.

Does this work? I know I personally find this approach distasteful and unhelpful – I would prefer to see politicians showing a modicum of respect for their rivals and inform us how they will best support us.

Casting the competitive nature of politics to one side, I can think of one or two other examples where this idea of collaboration does work well.

What about one of my favourite TV programmes, *The Apprentice*? Currently in its 16th season, this programme consistently demonstrates that whilst all the contestants are competing for one prize, they initially stand the best chance of winning the prize by working as a team. They can only progress when they win the team challenge every week.

I do think sometimes, like the contestants on *The Apprentice*, the field of NLP is quite inward-looking and tends to focus in on the NLP community rather than outwards at the general public. If a lot of the public have not yet heard of NLP, then it probably isn't going to be within their range of options when they are facing a particular challenge.

So what could happen, if we started working together from the point of view that NLP needs to be noticed and recognised as a viable option first? Many of the NLP Professionals I speak with want to make a difference in the world, which is probably an aspiration for us all. So in the following scenario, I deliberately use an over emphasised example to illustrate my point.

Let's future pace and imagine, just for a moment, we have reached the stage where everyone in the UK now knows NLP is a credible solution for their particular problem...

Let's assume your ideal business model is to be seeing two clients a day, i.e. 10 clients a week, and you take only four weeks' holiday every year. Let's also assume the average client likes to have the equivalent of 10 NLP coaching sessions. Now let's be generous and assume even though the whole UK population (currently almost 68 million, and rising) knows about NLP, only half of them want to hire an NLP Professional for 10 sessions.

So how long would it take you to coach half the UK population? It would take you 625,000 years to coach half the UK population (i.e. 34,000,000 people × 10 sessions ÷ [48 weeks × 10 clients per week] = 70,000 years).

What if you are a trainer? Perhaps your ideal business model is to run four NLP training courses a year, with 250 people on each course (you may as well think big.). It would take you a mere 34,000 years to train half the population (i.e. 30,000,000 people ÷ [250 per course × 4 per year] = 34,000 years)…and this is only to Practitioner level.

Now, unless you have discovered the secret to eternal life, this just isn't going to happen with you working on your own. So, given we really do believe NLP can make a difference, then perhaps this example blows out any lurking scarcity belief and emphasises the need to work together.. As NLP continues to become more widely recognised, then everyone can take a share in the increased demand for our services.

At least this way, by acknowledging there is plenty of potential business to go around, we could collectively coach half the UK population a little more quickly, because I don't want to wait 70,000 years before the social impact of NLP really does start making a difference to society.

Even with this abundance reframe, NLP practitioners may still question why we would want to work together. Sometimes, greater things can be achieved as a team.

Think about the Team GB relay team who represent us in the Olympics. Our runners, as individuals, do not even reach the final of the 100 metres. But as a team, we can, and do win medals in the 100 metres relay finals because somehow, whatever the four runners put together as a team creates something which is more powerful and successful than each of them as individual runners.

Our Team GB relay runners certainly demonstrate the principle behind one of my favourite quotes by Mattie Stepanek (American poet, 1990–2004):

> Unity is strength…when there is teamwork and collaboration wonderful things can be achieved

Let's imagine, for a moment, there was a Team NLP, made up of every person who has ever invested in NLP and brought into the principle of the NLP Profession. So what great things could Team NLP achieve? What parts of the model could we adopt in order to make Team NLP succeed, and in the process, ensure every individual within Team NLP also enjoys success?

For a start, one of the things Team NLP would do is work as a team – just like in the relay, personal differences and squabbles are left behind once the race starts and everyone does work as a team when it counts. There may be squabbles along the way – golly, my brother and I used to fight like cat and dog when we were children. But when he got knocked out at school one day (not by me, I hasten to add), and was rushed to hospital, all those squabbles, disagreements and arguments were forgotten and we really pulled together as a family to make sure he was OK.

If we really need convincing about the value of teamwork, just remember how communities pull together, both in times of adversity, and also to achieve great things. This is often drawn to our attention when there is some sort of disaster, such as an earthquake or hurricane…or pandemic! There was an outpouring of support for the NHS during lockdown, which was started by one individual, Annemarie Plas, and gathered momentum as a way of showing our support.

Throughout lockdown, we stood on our doorstep every Thursday evening and made a noise for the NHS – my clapping alone would have made very little difference, and when pooled with the rest of our family and our neighbours up and down the road, we were heard. More importantly it gave us a small sense of belonging and connecting during surreal times; we checked in with our neighbours each week (from an appropriate distance of course).

Team NLP could model this camaraderie and team spirit to elevate NLP to the next level.

Think about a large corporation for a moment…one which employs thousands of people and has many different departments. It's a fairly safe bet that on occasions, there is in-house squabbling between departments, and there will be times when Sales disagrees with Marketing, Finance have an argument with Admin and everyone falls out with HR.

Whatever the internal disagreements, you can be fairly certain as far as the public face of the company is concerned, it presents a united front where everything appears to be harmonious and runs smoothly. The public front of the company is usually what the public will be buying into, so it is important it looks good, from the outside at least.

We all recognise more damage is done when individuals 'wash their dirty linen in public', as my grandma used to say. The same applies to NLP Professionals. If an NLP practitioner is ranting about perceived wrongs on social media, rather than approaching the alleged perpetrator direct, this is unprofessional behaviour and does nothing to enhance the public image of NLP.

I personally think it's vital that some of our other NLP colleagues consider the consequences of their actions on the field and think more carefully about sharing their divisive views in a public arena – NLP is not yet strong enough to withstand so much internal division aired in public. Individuals in the NLP field are concerned about the impact of Wikipedia or news articles that are less than complimentary about NLP – when actually, a lot of the content for these divisive stories are provided by the NLP community in the first place.

The same applies to NLP as a profession. As NLP Professionals, we could do our bit to chunk up and ensure NLP, as a whole, is recognised by the public as a viable alternative, at which point we can each step up as individuals and offer to play our part.

Working collaboratively does have an effect at every level. Life is about teamwork and I would suggest collaboration ultimately plays a part in every success. So it is really important to recognise and nurture the teams which have a role in your life, including your:

- Inner team.
- Role with clients.
- Role within the NLP profession.

Your inner team

The Team we sometimes overlook when thinking about teamwork is our inner team – all those things which play a part in our own physical, mental emotional and spiritual well-being. There are the obvious ways of nurturing our own inner team – ensuring we eat a healthy diet; addressing physical issues like aches and pains; ensuring we get sufficient rest and treating our bodies with care; making sure we take downtime for relaxation and mental rejuvenation and creating regular time out for ourselves.

John Seymour introduces the concept of the Seven Practices of Transformational NLP (Seymour, 2009), which he identified after noticing some of his NLP students seemed to get far greater benefit out of their NLP than others. He acknowledges there is a difference between inter-personal skills, i.e. communication between people, and intra-personal skills, i.e. communication within a person, and suggests it is the intra-personal skills which are the essential ones for personal development and transformational learning.

TIP

Take at least 2 hours a week to nurture your inner team and make sure you pause for long enough to review your practices and ensure your own physical, mental, emotional and spiritual needs are being met.

We do know the principles of putting ourselves first on occasions, and at least remembering we are part of the equation. I have been reminded, more than once, of the life jacket principle – if you are ever caught on the sinking ship, it is very important to put a life jacket on yourself first, because this way, you are then in a much better position to be able to help your family, or the others around you. After all, you are not likely to be much help to them if you end up sinking first.

The trick is then getting the right balance between looking after ourselves and looking after others…and that's another story.

Your role with clients

The teamwork you are possibly most familiar with is the team you create with your clients as you coach and support them to achieve their intended outcomes. No doubt we can all recollect occasions when we have really experienced this sense of teamwork when working with a client, or with our own coach.

I am privileged to be just a small cog in the ANLP Team. Even though we work remotely, we stay in regular contact with each other (thank goodness for WhatsApp, phones and Zoom) and we always have each other's backs. I would like to think we empower each other to be the best we can be and certainly, when we do all find ourselves together, for the conference and team days, we have a brilliant time together…which positively reflects on how we serve our community.

We do witness this sort of teamwork all the time and acknowledge sometimes it does take someone else to bring out the best in us. When I met my husband, Kash, I was joyously catapulted into a whole new level of teamwork. He knows how to push me, support me, stand behind me, beside me or in front of me, depending on what is required at the time. He is my foundation for flying and my soft place to land – maybe that makes him my cushion, though I know he is so much more than that! He has certainly taken me on a joyous journey of self-discovery, and shown me how to make the best of myself with what I already have…talk about helping us to discover the hidden resources we all have within us.

A scenario I am sure many of you are familiar with is working with an NLP Coach. A successful coaching relationship is very much a team-based approach and I know how much I benefit from working with my own coach, who both challenges me and supports me in equal measure!

Your role within the NLP profession

So what exactly is teamwork in the field? Am I talking about the team created between the shepherd, the sheepdog and the flock of sheep, as they successfully move smoothly seamlessly from one end of the field to a pen at the other end? Not quite, although this does work as an example of teamwork.

There are many professional fields, other than those which readily spring to mind. Actors form part of a profession, and even when one actor wins an Oscar, there is a whole team of people they usually thank for helping them get as far as the winner's podium.

Let's face it, for starters, they first have to have starred in a film in order to be noticed and nominated for an Oscar. And we all know, from the rolling credits at the end of every film, just how many hundreds of people play a part in getting this actor onto our cinema screen.

And what about our own professional field, i.e. the field of NLP. Remember Team NLP? We all belong to Team NLP by virtue of the fact we have had training in NLP. Some of us may be more active team players than others and we all have a part to play in developing and nurturing and protecting the NLP profession.

This is where the professional bodies and/or trade associations come in. Most professions do have a professional body (or two) – solicitors have the Law Society, doctors have the British Medical Association (BMA) and accountants successfully operate with a framework of more than one professional body, such as the Institute of Chartered Accountants, the Chartered Institute of Management Accountants and the Association of Chartered Certified Accountants.

The main benefit of the professional bodies and trade associations is the added value they give to the profession as a whole. They can act as the collective voice on behalf of their members and ensure members are represented when it matters, i.e. in the regulation debate, with standards setting and with accreditation.

ANLP has a great working relationship with the other three main globally recognised associations: International NLP Trainers Association (INLPTA), The International Association for NLP (IANLP) and the International Association for NLP Institutes (IN). The associations call their NLP Team the Talking Circle of Associations (TCA) and the leaders of these Associations regularly collaborate, converse and work together on key projects for the good of the NLP Community (Collaborating Associations, 2020). This relationship was borne out of mutual respect and shared values and goes from strength to strength.

When I was an accountant, I used to belong to the Federation of Small Businesses (FSB) and as a landlord, the National Residential Landlords Association (NRLA). I did get some benefits of membership, such as free business banking, a credit card and a free legal helpline!

What had – and has – more value for me, however, is representation and a say when things happened which could affect me as a small businesses or property owner. I always fill out the surveys which come from both the FSB and the NRLA, because this was my way of having a voice, and lending my support to the collective voice of small businesses and landlords.

For example, the FSB stand a much greater chance of successfully lobbying parliament about issues affecting small businesses if they can say they surveyed their members and that out of 300,000 responses, 87% of small businesses are concerned about the effect of increasing petrol prices or have been adversely affected by the change in employment law.

As one small business in the UK, I'm sure I would have to write an awful lot of letters to my MP and various cabinet ministers to have the same collective impact as the FSB...and I know parliament would talk to the FSB to seek their opinion and the opinion of their members. To put this into perspective, the government would need a pretty huge table if they were to consider inviting me and every other small business in the UK (which make up 95% of British businesses) to a round table discussion about the effects of their latest proposed business legislation.

TIP

Join some of the social NLP Groups on LinkedIn and start contributing to the group dynamic.

It is important to acknowledge the benefits of building strategic alliances, partnering with others for specific purposes or projects. ANLP have built many Strategic Alliances within the NLP Community and certainly enjoy building teams, partnerships and relationships in order to create value for others. As an unregulated field, it is both important and significant the professional bodies like ANLP work with universities and regulatory bodies to explore opportunities for NLP Professionals; ANLP engages with the NLP community to report successes and share applications of NLP through their *Rapport* Magazine their annual conference and their NLP Awards. They work with the certifying bodies to develop guidelines for the NLP Community, such as Master Trainers criteria and introduce like-minded people within the community to encourage the sharing of resources, and work collaboratively to support and develop their ideas for a particular sector of society. They do all of this and play a large part of the emerging professional field for NLP.

They are simply modelling strategic alliances which happen successfully elsewhere on a wider scale. Think about the North Atlantic Treaty Organisation (NATO), the World Health Organisation (WHO) and the United Nations (UN).

I am sure you can think of models which would work within the NLP community. Wouldn't it be fun to chunk up and apply some NLP to the community, rather than always focusing on the individuals within it?

How about some Time Line work, so any negative feelings from the past can be acknowledged and the useful learnings taken from those past events and applied now?

What about some parts integration work to discover the positive intention behind the divisions and heal the conflicts of the past?

How about we all adopt the presuppositions of NLP and apply these to the community as well as to ourselves?

Ooooohhh, the possibilities are endless, and the great thing is, we already know about them. So collectively, it could be quite simple to make these things happen.

Summary

By reframing things as an NLP Professional, and starting to view NLP as the team to which we all belong, the reasons for collaborating and working with others become more apparent.

By working collaboratively, we can collectively take responsibility for raising the profile of NLP, getting it more widely accepted as a profession and pool our resources so NLP is noticed for the right reasons.

Actions

Make contact with and introduce yourself to at least one other NLP Professional in your local area. Just be curious and be open to the possibilities that might arise when you explore potential avenues for working collaboratively.

*• an annual turnover of £10.2 million or less;
 • total fixed and current assets on its balance sheet of £5.1 million or less; and
 • 50 employees or less.

123

CHAPTER 7
Raising Awareness of NLP

'The first step toward change is awareness.
The second step is acceptance.'
Nathaniel Branden, psychotherapist

Even with the efforts of individual practitioners, training schools and organisations like ANLP, NLP is still not widely recognised as a credible solution to many of life's challenges.

There are many reasons for this already covered in previous chapters, and these cumulate in a lack of understanding about what NLP is and how it can help an individual.

NLP Professionals recognise the need to raise awareness of NLP by effective marketing and they embrace every opportunity to raise the profile of NLP. NLP Professionals understand by raising the profile of NLP, they are ultimately increasing demand for their services as an NLP Professional. NLP Professionals allocate a budget for marketing and realise it is an essential part of their overall business strategy.

In their book *Neuro-Linguistic Programming: A Critical Appreciation for Managers and Developers* (Tosey, 2009), Paul Tosey and Jane Mathison identified that NLP is at a crossroads and has so far failed to become accepted as a mainstream practice. They cite the factional nature as being one of the issues which has contributed to this failure, and perhaps it is true we don't always have the best role models in NLP.

So apart from recognising we could all take on board our own presuppositions and pay more attention to respecting other people's model of the world, where does this leave us now? The past is the past, and we are where we are now. We, as Professionals in NLP, collectively hold the power to shape our own future and the future of our field.

It could be helpful to understand more about the bigger picture around how people make their decisions when evaluating NLP as a potential solution. This information could be used to identify ways in which we, as a community could work together to encourage more people to choose NLP as the natural solution to their particular problem, alongside other alternatives such as cognitive behavioural therapy (CBT).

As CEO of ANLP, I hear the voices of the public on a daily basis and they talk with us about their perceptions of NLP as a profession because we are in a position to be able to offer impartial and independent advice.

Since ANLP personnel are not actually offering their services to callers as a practitioner or as a trainer, the public also talk about their challenges when looking for an NLP professional, and the issues they face when they want to make a decision about getting some help for their particular issue.

I have consolidated some of these voices to benefit the NLP community because the main benefit from generating more interest in NLP would be a bigger pool of potential clients for you.

I am keen to share this information because like you, I want you to be successful as an NLP Professional. After all, we, as the NLP Community, are only going to make a big difference to society if we all recognise, value and accept our own important and individual contribution to the field of NLP.

There are some key areas into which I have grouped these observations around how the public make their decisions and choose NLP.

To create a more professional field for NLP, I suggest everyone has a part to play in:

- Ensuring NLP is one of the obvious natural solutions chosen by the public when they have a problem.

- Changing the public perception of NLP so they find it easier to make this choice.

- Appreciating the importance of reputation.

Before looking at these points in detail, it might serve as a useful reminder to consider how people make decisions. I have already talked about the concept of NLP Professionals offering solutions to specific problems and this pattern does emerge in the bigger picture concept of decision making (rather than the detail of a decision making strategy). For now, let's call this the Decision Tree.

Decision Tree

The Decision Tree starts with a problem or question which a member of the public needs to address. I think it would be easier to use an example to illustrate this, so the one I am going to use is smoking. The problem is that this person – let's call them Sam – smokes and they want to stop smoking (not the best phrase from an NLP perspective, and one which is universally recognised).

So, Sam has decided they want to stop smoking and the first thing they would like to do is identify all the potential solutions or aids which could be useful in helping them. Let's assume they have already decided they are not confident they can do this on their own and they want some additional support along the way.

Sam now has a number of options to consider. Do they use nicotine patches, hypnosis or NLP? In fact, it turns out there are many different solutions available, including counselling, CBT, emotional

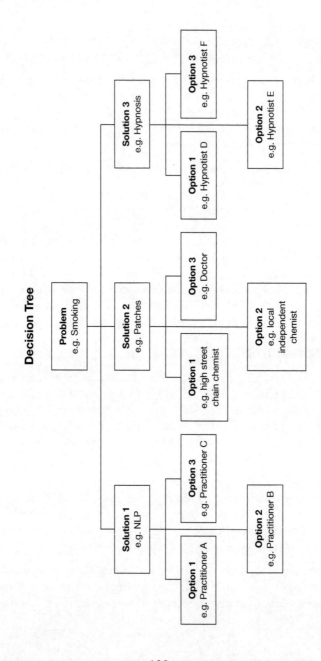

Decision Tree

freedom technique (EFT) and homeopathy...so how do they decide which one to choose?

Sam is likely to be attracted to the option which captures their attention most powerfully – by the beacon which is shining brightest, the voice which is singing the sweetest song, or the emotion which tugs them most strongly.

And Sam will also rely upon the signposts out there, guiding them in one direction or another. These guides could influence them by pointing them in a particular direction and helping them to make a decision about whether to choose patches, or hypnosis or NLP. These guides, or facilitators are external influences and will include the internet, the NHS and the relevant associations or representative bodies.

Once Sam has decided on which particular path to take, they will then choose the specific solution to get them there. So, if they decide to use nicotine patches to help them quit smoking, then they will decide whether to get these from their GP, high street chain chemist, or their local independent chemist.

And if they choose NLP, they will then choose the Professional who is most likely to satisfy their particular requirements. And at this stage, they will still be attracted by the beacon which is shining brightest, the voice which is singing the sweetest song, or the emotion which tugs them most strongly – and this time it will be on a more specific level.

Of course, it is also possible for Sam to come across a Professional who is able to help with their challenge, only to discover afterwards that NLP was the name of the tool being used. And this is absolutely fine, both ways of attracting a potential client work well and can be effective.

TIP

Use the Decision Tree model to help define your niche and define your own shining beacon of light.

However, this understanding of the bigger picture Decision Tree, could be harnessed and used alongside existing individual marketing strategies, to leverage things in favour of NLP.

So what effect does this Decision Tree have in ensuring NLP is one of the natural solutions chosen by the public when they have a problem? What does this have to do with changing the public perception of NLP so they know how to make a more informed choice more easily? And what is your personal role in all this?

To go back to my original comments about us all having a part to play…

Ensuring NLP is one of *the* natural solutions chosen by the public when they have a problem

It seems one of the challenges we face as an NLP community is the brightness of our light, the sweetness of our voice and the strength of our emotional tug – in other words, our power to attract. If people do not even see NLP as an option for dealing with their particular problem, then NLP will not be their natural solution.

Whilst awareness of NLP is increasing, we have already established there is still room for improvement. We are still not at the point where NLP is always considered the first choice for someone like Sam who wants to quit smoking. Our beacon is not shining brightly enough.

My personal view is that I see the NLP community as being a bit like a secret garden. We have a vast array of wonderful things to offer and between us we cover every single element you could possibly want in a garden. We have bountiful vegetable patches, beautiful rose gardens, practical areas for BBQing, areas where we can simply sit and enjoy, fun areas for playing and areas for being curious, a nursery garden for baby plants and even test beds for creating new species or improving the viability of existing species.

Yet most of this is well hidden, just like a secret garden, because, as a community, we have not yet succeeded in working together to present this beautiful garden to the public in a way which they can then enjoy it and benefit from it.

Sometimes NLP has had a bad press, and what weakens the NLP message even further, and keeps it little known, is when NLP practitioners use NLP and relabel it to avoid any negative reactions. The result is that NLP is being used to achieve success, and the success is being attributed to something other than NLP.

As a community of like-minded people, we already understand the benefits of NLP because we have directly experienced them. I'm pretty certain we would be doing something else if we hadn't experienced some positive results from using NLP ourselves, so we already know what are talking about.

However, despite being skilled in the art of communication, we do not always communicate the benefits of NLP in a way which makes it easier for the public to understand how effective NLP could be as the solution to their issue.

As I have mentioned previously, one of the keys to successfully promoting NLP is to use examples where your clients have experienced success using NLP to deal with a particular challenge, issue or problem.

These do need to be communicated in a way that is easily understood. This narrative evidence (success stories, case studies or testimonials) can be written in such a way so that someone facing a similar challenge could empathise and understand how NLP was able to help with overcoming the issue.

Most importantly, these stories need to focus on how NLP has made a practical and understandable difference to someone's life. Think about what your potential client will be able to empathise with and understand, rather than what you want to tell them.

If you were, for a moment, to step into the shoes of a member of the public, considering NLP as a possible solution to your particular issue (let's just say you want to stop smoking), which of these two statements would be more appealing to you?

131

A. My name is George. I am an INPLTA ITA ABNLP SNLP NLPU NLP Practitioner based in Kent. I have trained all over the world with Richard Bandler, Wyatt Woodsmall, Robert Dilts, John Grinder and Tad James. I specialise in helping people stop smoking and I have been very successful in this area.

B. My name is Jo. I was smoking 40 a day. I had tried all sorts of things to help me stop smoking and nothing seemed to work. Before I went to see George, an NLP Professional, I would get short of breath and I could no longer run around the park with my kids. Smoking was ruining my life. As a result of the strategies taught to me by George, I have now chosen to quit smoking and have not had a cigarette for over six months now – I feel a lot better now I have been able to make this decision and my children seem much happier too because they now have a dad who keeps up with them in the park.

Statement A is all about George and how fabulous he is as a Practitioner. It tells you very little about how George was able to help and what difference NLP (and George) actually made to the client. It assumes the reader (i.e. potential client) already knows about NLP and how it can help, and all it really does is tell us about gorgeous George.

Statement B, on the other hand, is far more specific and focused on the effects of the presenting problem and solution. It informs the reader (potential client) how NLP has helped and what a difference it has made. It provides a story to which someone with a similar fear may just relate.

So, if you were a member of the public who did want to quit smoking, I wonder which story would be more likely to motivate you into taking some action. And which just might generate enough interest get into the local paper next time a journalist is searching for examples of smoking related success stories. I suspect it would be Jo's story of how he quit smoking with the help of an NLP Professional (Example B).

TIP

Prepare some short promotional success stories/case
studies of your own. Top and tail these when relevant
and use as press releases for local news media.

Whilst you are quite rightly proud of your achievements and the
work you have had to put in to become a top rate NLP Professional,
the public don't really know much about the different training
organisations or certification bodies. And with all due respect to
Richard Bandler and John Grinder, had you actually heard of them
before you got involved with NLP?

So would you agree it is in all our best interests to promote the
practical applications, positive experiences and benefits of NLP to
the public first? This way, there is a natural and believable counter-
balance to the negative press, and the public are more inclined to
visit the NLP garden rather than the CBT garden or the hypnotherapy garden. We can then start to ensure NLP is one of *the* natural
solutions chosen by the public when they have a problem.

Changing the public perception of NLP so they find it easier to make this choice

As I mentioned earlier, I am lucky enough to talk to the public on
a daily basis and they are usually those people who have, one way
or another, discovered NLP could be the solution to their particular
challenge.

So why are they contacting ANLP rather than going directly to the
practitioner or trainer who will help them with their problem? It
seems there are three main reasons, which crop up again and again
during these conversations. Generally it seems the public contact
us because they are:

1. Confused.
2. Overwhelmed.
3. Seeking reassurance.

So let's break these down a bit further:

- **Confused**. The public are confused because there is no clear signposting within NLP.

  I spoke to a lovely lady recently who said she had decided to call ANLP 'as a last resort' because she still had no clear idea what would be the best training route for her. She explained she had already spoken to a number of trainers, and said they were all willing to help.

  But what she actually wanted first was to understand more about NLP per se, why she should consider NLP training, what were the training certification routes and what could be the consequences in choosing one certification body over another. She wanted to understand this before she could start to make a decision about which specific trainer to choose. She was just doing her due diligence about NLP before she was ready to choose the right NLP Trainer. So I sent her various links to resources and information on the ANLP website, which helped her to complete her research.

  Another person I spoke to recently was confused about the acronyms and what they actually meant. Would it be 'better' for him to choose INLPTA, ABNLP or an SNLP approved trainer and which one, if any, was the overarching certification body for NLP?

  NLP is full of jargon and acronyms. NLP may have a great meaning for us, and in reality, what does Neuro Linguistic Programming really mean to the man (or woman) on the street?

  I never really appreciated how challenging acronyms and jargon could be to other people until I became a school governor. Here I was, a reasonably educated and intelligent adult, moving into the world of education, which is absolutely full of acronyms. I must have sat in the first two or three meetings completely oblivious to what was actually being said, because

I was so busy making notes of all the acronyms I needed to google later.

Let's be honest here for a moment: as a community we understand our own history and on occasions seem to be happy to model our founders and create division within our community. In the past, we have created divisions between the 7-day and 20-day practitioners; or those who have trained through INLPTA, The Professional Guild, SNLP, ABNLP, ITA. It's confusing for anyone on the outside of our community looking in, because they don't know where to start.

Again, if we are being really honest for a moment, as a community, there are still calls in some sectors to agree a universal definition for NLP, or even one which is widely accepted in the UK. I once put out a call on LinkedIn, asking for an easily accessible and universally understood definition of NLP and managed to gather over 30 definitions within two days – all valid and clearly stated, and all different.

TIP

Create a clear definition of NLP to put on your own website...and make sure it is one which is understood by the general public. Or feel free to use this one, reproduced from the ANLP website:

NLP combines theories, models and techniques from a range of scientific and esoteric fields, to create accessible, understandable 'tools' which can be used by individuals, teams and organisations and applied in a variety of contexts to improve outcomes, support wellbeing and create change

So, if it has been a challenge to nail a definition of NLP, think how confusing it must be for the general public to work out what NLP could do for them. NLP can be so hard to define in simple terms, maybe it would be more useful to use examples rather than definitions.

At least there is a well-defined certification structure in NLP (i.e. Practitioner, Master Practitioner, Trainer) and as a result of opening the Pandora's box about Trainers' Training, ANLP facilitated a collaboration between all the main certifying bodies represented in the UK, before producing a clear set of criteria for achieving Master Trainer status.

If we, as a community have a bit of confusion around defining NLP, clarifying the certification structure and where to create a focal point for NLP, it's not surprising the public, looking into our garden for the first time, could be equally confused as to where they start.

- **Overwhelmed.** The public are overwhelmed because there is so much choice.

To go back to our garden analogy, at the moment we have every single flower, vegetable and piece of hard landscaping in our garden, which is superb, especially for an options person like me. But this choice can be completely overwhelming for someone coming into the garden for the first time, who is not a gardening expert and who cannot tell the difference between a *Quercus* and a *Daucus carota* (an oak tree and a carrot).

And it's even more confusing because all these plants are everywhere in the garden. Carrots sit alongside roses and blackberries grow on top of these, because they are all vying for attention.

Everyone in the garden wants to be noticed, this is understandable...and in our eagerness to be noticed, perhaps we forget there are lots of other gardens for people to choose from, so we could end up putting people off our garden altogether, especially if they are not yet convinced NLP is the right garden to be in.

Remember, NLP does not yet have the same universal understanding as, say, supermarkets. Everyone, yes everyone, knows the benefits of supermarket shopping, so the supermarkets can afford to vie for our attention by directly criticising their competition (Aldi's baked beans are cheaper than Tesco this week).

The same cannot be said for NLP yet, so there is everything to gain by the NLP Community working together to develop the big picture plan for promoting NLP to the public and getting people into our garden (or supermarket) first.

- **Seeking reassurance.** The public want to know the NLP garden is a safe garden to enter.

   NLP, like coaching and many other personal development methodologies, is currently unregulated, so increasingly the public are looking for reassurance from somewhere. Understandably, they want to know that if they choose to come into the NLP garden, they will be protected.

   People want to believe their investment in your services will have a positive effect on their lives. It can be a huge investment for them, both in terms of time and financial commitment, so they do want to believe it will work.

   Obviously, as a subjective experience, a lot does depend on their attitude and whether or not they are ready to make the necessary changes. But for them to make this choice in the first place, it does help if they have heard or read something positive about NLP.

   NLP training and NLP consultations are quite an investment of someone's hard earned money, and they do want guarantees it is going to be money well spent.

So if we were to work together to address these concerns of confusion, overwhelm and reassurance, we could start changing the public perception of NLP so they find it easier to choose NLP.

Appreciating the importance of reputation

The other thing which needs to be addressed when considering raising the profile of NLP is the importance of reputation.

Leaping off a tower in front of my children probably increased their respect for me and my reputation with them, albeit temporarily (see earlier reference!). Integrity and trust are an important part of the relationship you build with your clients, and they also contribute to your reputation. I am sure you, like me, prefer to purchase goods and services which have either been recommended, or come from a reputable source…and I am sure, like me, you have become more reliant on reviews in recent years, because it is so much easier to access them.

Building your reputation in NLP can work in two ways…you can either use your existing reputation to build your business or use your business success to build your reputation.

A great example of using your existing reputation to build your NLP business is Zoe Carroll, a former teacher who is now working with East Sussex College Group as a consultant, using NLP to build confidence in teenagers, especially around aspirations and exam success. Zoe has harnessed her existing good reputation as a successful teacher to build her NLP business.

On the other hand, NLP Trainer, Robbie Steinhouse, used his previous business success to build a reputation as an NLP coach and trainer. He walked away from an executive role in his recruitment business in 2002 to set up his NLP Coaching and Training business, NLP School. He focused on offering coaching and training in a corporate environment and followed this up with a series of books aimed at business leaders and entrepreneurs.

Reputation takes time to build up and yet can be destroyed in moments. Just look at the scandals which have haunted various figures in the public eye in recent years. For example, Kevin Spacey, one of the best actors around and star of many box office hit movies, had his career ruined overnight in 2017, when allegations were made around sexual misconduct (he subsequently pleaded guilty to charges in 2018).

When we individually and collectively raise the positive reputation of NLP, we will improve its credibility. Then we will all be in a much better position to benefit from the increased demand for the services of NLP Professionals.

There are real benefits to creating positive PR around NLP as a viable solution and therefore raising the profile of NLP as a Profession.

There is a saying 'any publicity is good publicity', and perhaps this depends more on your motives and outcome for generating the publicity in the first place. There are certain reality TV celebrities who do seem to believe this, and we are just as likely to read about something terrible they have done as we are to read about their latest success.

Is it possible to measure the impact of PR? It probably depends on the intended outcome. Whilst a newsworthy story raises your profile, I would suggest a positive one increases your business success.

Patrick Cordell, who won the NLP in Education Award at the 2017 NLP Awards, was able to use his winning success to his advantage, as part of his pitch to secure lottery funding.

The more positive news people can read about NLP, the more it does become a credible option for them. Even if, at the time they read about it, they don't have any specific reason for wanting to engage the services of an NLP Professional, the information may filter into their subconscious and stay there, ready to be recalled at a later date when it is needed.

Publicity, good and bad, ripples outwards, just like the drops of rain landing on a still pond. We know how the communication model works, so it is in our interests to ensure the NLP related messages stored away for future reference are positive ones. This way NLP becomes one of the credible options which is considered when the time is right.

TIP

We all know about cause and effect, and how it can be much more useful for us to be 'at cause'. So take 100% responsibility for building a good reputation for NLP.

To ensure NLP continues to improve its reputation, we could start to consider the impact of the messages we send out. Again, we know about the communication model and the way we filter and store information in our unconscious mind.

One person who probably does understand the full implication of the communication model and maintaining a good reputation is Gerald Ratner. It may have been 1991 when he made his now infamous speech to the Institute of Directors, and called his own products, from Ratners the jewellers, 'crap' and yet this is still a pertinent example today. This was a joke he had made many times before, and on this occasion, it was reported by the *Daily Mirror*, who implied he was making fun of his own customers.

As a result of this speech, Ratners' shares plummeted, the business suffered and Gerald Ratner lost his job as Chief Executive and Chairman of the world's biggest jewellery company. One word became very costly for the man who had once enjoyed a six-figure salary and chauffeur-driven limousines.

The world has changed considerably since 1991, and the internet has made everything more accessible to everyone. Today, it's more likely that Gerald Ratner would get into trouble by writing his observations on the internet or social media, just as Elon Musk tends to do fairly regularly, sometimes with disastrous consequences. The power of the misplaced tweet comment by Elon Musk has been known to wipe millions off the value of stocks and shares and crash cryptocurrency, which may not impact on him and I am sure there have been consequences for others in the same arena.

It seems today everyone has an online presence and raises their profile with social media marketing. We tweet and blog and post our comments on Facebook and LinkedIn, and probably on many other easily accessible online media platforms.

The whole world can, if they choose, read our comments and views about NLP and find out about our heated debates and disagreements and distasteful and personal comments about other NLP practitioners, which sometimes seem to be deliberately designed to shock and fire up debate.

I have even dealt with complaints made by members of the public (against non ANLP members), who are aghast when the details of their private lives or their particular issue have been openly debated, ridiculed and commented upon within an online forum...sometimes without even changing the name of the client.

So we don't necessarily need a newspaper to expose these things nowadays because if any practitioner chooses to write detrimental comments about NLP or the people within our community, they are there, on the internet, for all to see...and this can have a knock-on effect for the reputation of NLP as a whole.

TIP

Think about who is going to read your comments before you post them on the internet for your potential clients to read.

Summary

When the public become more aware NLP is a solution to their problem, then they will start to appreciate you could be the NLP Professional to help them. As awareness increases, so does acceptance, and as NLP becomes more widely accepted, there will be increased demands for your services as an NLP Professional.

Actions

Write at least one success story which is relevant to your niche and use this to promote your services and obtain some extra PR via local media (radio, magazines and newspapers,). Remember to send it in to *Rapport* Magazine too for inclusion in a future issue of the magazine for NLP Professionals!

CHAPTER 8

Dispelling Some Common Myths in NLP

'You must be the change you want to see in the world'
Mahatma Gandhi, Lawyer and non-violent revolutionary

NLP practitioners often come across various myths relating to the field of NLP and can often been seen to be perpetuating these myths further by their own practices.

Of course, NLP professionals are well equipped to dispel these myths with narrative evidence…and of course, we are also empowered to change our own limiting beliefs, that we may have inherited or been influenced by outside of the NLP Community.

Let's be clear – a 'myth', in this instance, is defined as 'a commonly believed but false idea (Definition of Myth, 2022)

Top of the agenda of NLP myths could be the various less than helpful terms that NLP has been associated with in the past. At various times, NLP has been referred to as:

- a cult
- manipulative

- a cure
- a pseudoscience

So let's start with dispelling these myths before moving on...

Is NLP a cult?

A cult is variously defined as 'a particular system of religious worship, especially with reference to its rites or ceremonies' or a' a group or sect bound together by veneration of the same thing, person, ideal etc' or 'an instance of great veneration of a person, ideal or thing, especially as manifested by a body of admirers'.

Paul Tosey and Jane Mathison dispel any ideas of NLP being a cult in *Neuro-Linguistic Programming, A Critical Appreciation for Managers and Developers* (Chapter 13), not only because according to the International Cultic Studies Association, the word cult is prone to be used to imply disrepute, and also by the very fact that NLP Practitioners have huge freedom to do what they want when they want – they are not locked away in a commune somewhere, having denounced their friends, family and chattels and paying their dues to a leading master somewhere. As Tosey and Mathison say 'concerns voiced about NLP as a "cult" wither in the face of serious scrutiny'.

Having worked with Paul (Tosey) and Jane (Mathison) in the past, I respect their views and know that they are well thought through and considered. Whilst I know NLP has been referred to as a cult in the past, thankfully, these views are now in the past...if ever there were any figures within the NLP community that cultivated a cult status (deliberate choice of words), they have been replaced by those who firmly believe that NLP is a positive solution and can demonstrate this fact – this makes them passionate about what they do, just as I am. Having a passionate belief in what you do is very different from the mind control exerted by cult leaders.

Is NLP manipulative?

As NLP Professionals, we do recognise that any form of communication could be perceived as being manipulative – after all, 'you cannot *not* communicate'. You only have to watch a child with their parents or grandparents to know all there is to know about the art of manipulation…and I bet not many children have ever read a book about NLP.

I have experienced many occasions in a business context where one person has got their way through sulking or shouting or generally being louder, or indeed quieter, than everyone else! Most of us will have witnessed people playing out strategies for manipulating others to get their desired outcome. As Tosey and Mathison state, 'NLP can offer a radical challenge to some "common sense" assumptions about language, communication and behaviour. At best, NLP can raise people's awareness of how they might be influencing other people, educates them and encourages them to be more responsible for the effects they have on other people.'

NLP has specifically garnered a reputation for being manipulative because there are some practitioners who have deliberately positioned NLP as a manipulative tool for seduction, unscrupulous sales techniques and mind control. I did a quick search on Amazon for manipulation techniques and came up with some interesting books linking NLP manipulation with dark psychology.

All this means is that some practitioners have created their business from these applications of NLP, in just the same way that other professions have niches that may not serve their profession that well – ambulance-chasing lawyers, for example; the marketing businesses that make money by selling your details (despite the introduction of DPA(2018) regulations); online betting apps who entice gamblers with offers of free bets; and what about doctors like Crippin and Shipman, who certainly did a disservice to their profession?

However, as Tosey and Mathison say, this actually 'escalates rather than diminishes the level of ethical responsibility on the trained practitioner. Once we accept the principle that we cannot not influence other people through our communication, it becomes more problematic to distinguish between appropriate and inappropriate influence'.

NLP is not manipulative and some NLP practitioners are, because they use their language skills deliberately and knowingly to coerce and persuade others to their way of thinking. This reflects on poor practices from certain people in the field, rather than on NLP itself.

Is NLP a cure?

One of the challenges faced in NLP is when it is positioned by some as being a 'cure' for everything. 'Cure' is defined as either 'to make someone with an illness healthy again' or 'to solve a problem'.

There is increasing neurological evidence of a mind–body connection and this research has enabled us to better relate the positive impact of NLP, when related to medical conditions and when solving problems.

NLP is, at best, about learning to cultivate a positive mindset, adopting strategies that help us navigate life and ensure we can model excellence when we see examples of this in others. It is the NLP Professional, working collaboratively with their client, that facilitates the solutions…not NLP itself.

NLP is not a cream that can be applied to the sore spot until it miraculously heals itself! Anyone who seeks NLP as their cure could benefit from some education about what NLP can do to empower them to find a solution to their problem, rather than be applied to them in order to cure them.

Sitting alongside the claim that NLP is a cure, is the belief adopted by a few NLP practitioners, that they are omnipotent! I would argue that NLP creates *empowerment* rather than omnipotence… although in that revelatory moment, I guess the two could be easily confused. If you have potential clients who believe you can cure them, its important to remind them that they have a very large part to play in any changes they want in their life – you cannot do it for them.

Is NLP a pseudoscience?

This is one of the main claims made by those posting on Wikipedia. In fact, if you google NLP and pseudoscience, the top reference is Wikipedia and pretty much all the other references are NLP related websites, disputing the claim! The claim that NLP is a pseudo-science derives from the 'fact' that there is, allegedly, no research whatsoever to back it up.

However, as I mentioned in Chapter 4, if you visit the site, NLPWiki, you can actually download a 123-page NLP Research document citing all the references and abstracts for positive, direct and indirect published research for NLP. Whilst I have no intention of listing all the abstracts here, I would encourage you to visit the site and download this information, which is readily available to all who choose to seek it.

Remember, some of the greatest transformations from pseudoscience to science include

- the solar system (it was once believed that the sun orbited the earth, until Copernicus proved otherwise)
- the shape of earth (it was once believed the earth was flat, until a collection of people including Pythagoras and Aristotle, theorised that the earth was a sphere)

Agreed, in the beginning, Bandler and Grinder did tend to shy away from a research paradigm, and many since then have followed through and had research published in a number of peer-reviewed academically respected journals. With the advances in neuroscience research, many of the early modalities modelled in NLP are now being backed by the scientific evidence.

So there is enough evidence building to move on and change some of the ways NLP is viewed in the public domain.

Is the only valid NLP research clinically based?

It is often claimed that the efficacy and effectiveness of NLP can only be proved by undertaking clinical research and clinical trials.

Of course, as I said in Chapter 4, when NLP is being used in a clinical or therapeutic setting such as PTSD, in-depth research, including clinical trials, is incredibly important.

However, ANLP have developed an *Applications of NLP* model, which broadly divides NLP applications into 4 quadrants, *one* of which is Clinical/Therapeutic Interventions.

APPLICATIONS OF NLP

So what about the other 3 quadrants where NLP can be applied effectively and with great success? Whilst clinical trials and RCT's are essential in therapeutic application of NLP, are clinical trials really essential in these other areas? Are all techniques currently adopted in the fields of personal development, organisational development and education currently subjected to such rigorous testing?

We know they are not, so why should NLP be treated any differently to other widely adopted models in these sectors?

In these other areas narrative evidence, case studies and models are as important and more significant for demonstrating that NLP is an effective solution.

The BCG Matrix (Boston Consulting Group, Bruce Henderson, 1968), for example, is a well-respected model used in Management Consulting and is quoted widely as a reputable framework that helps organisations determine which areas of their business deserve more resources and investment. For those of you less familiar with it, it is the four-quadrant model also known as the Growth Share Matrix, which incorporates cash cows, dogs, stars and question marks.

The model was produced by studying (modelling) companies that had mainly done something innovative or well (mostly intuitively) around their product portfolio and which carried on doing it because it worked. Bruce Henderson at Boston Consulting Group, collated this information and produced the model in a simple, visual, four-quadrant format.

This model is applied widely in business in areas that can have a significant impact on the overall success of the organisation. The model is adapted depending on the client situation and context – and the underlying principles are the same as in 1968. The model itself is not questioned. It works.

So what about using NLP models in a similar way, introducing them as models to be adopted in personal, organisational and educational establishments because they work when applied in relevant contexts?

I have done this myself as a volunteer within the Scout Association, when I was asked to deliver one of the Leader training modules entitled Working with Adults, for our local Scout Leaders in Hemel Hempstead. The outcomes of the training were fairly straightforward and could all be achieved using NLP, so I asked if I could deviate from the training guides, as long as the outcomes were still met.

I was given permission to do so and so developed a simple two-hour training which demonstrated the Communication Model and

Perceptual Positions – with appropriate Scout-related examples and the chance to experience the models through practical work.

The demos, using Scout leaders and their real-life scenarios worked superbly every time, and the feedback, from adult leaders who were giving up a Saturday morning to complete mandatory training, was always positive:

'I've learned so much this morning that I can use in everyday life, not just Scouts.'

'Now I understand how those parents feel.'

'This is the most informative training I have ever attended.'

Because I presented these as NLP models that the Leaders could use if they worked for them, I was never asked about efficacy and clinical trials – why would I have been? These volunteers were just really happy to have been given some extra tools they could utilise in their roles as Scout Leaders…and in other areas of their lives.

My husband, Kash, introduced NLP into the local educational setting by undertaking a Geography department modelling project as part of his Master Practitioner certification. The Geography department at our school has consistently delivered above average GCSE results based upon national statistics, so of course, there was an ideal project in the making.

Kash carried out a standard NLP modelling project with the Geography department staff, eliciting a whole raft of strategies that they used to achieve these excellent results year after year. He distilled the results down into the differences that made the difference and from these results, created some tangible models that could be adopted by other departments.

Of course, in reality, there are many constraints within the education system that may create barriers to success in rolling out these models and, despite that, the school have acknowledged they do have some great models that they intend to roll out, one department at a time – small steps in the right direction, without any need for clinical research.

There are many different ways of collecting data to prove the efficacy of NLP. Asking questions, reframing and challenging beliefs is what we do, so I would encourage openness and a willingness around putting NLP through the same process which we put our clients…by recording the results.

There are levels of research which are acceptable, and not all research does have to be clinically rigorous, particularly in the realms where the scientific method is inappropriate. Cognitive behavioural therapy (CBT) is widely recognised within the NHS and one of the main reasons for this is because they record their results, and therefore have evidence a patient has made progress.

NLP interventions already measure results as well. Otherwise how would you know when a client has reached their outcome? How many times have you said to a client, before their NLP coaching: 'On a scale of 1 to 10, how do you feel about [your challenge] at the moment?'

And then once you have completed the NLP intervention or coaching session, you will ask the same question, so both you and your client can get an idea of where they are now with regard to their particular challenge.

So I would suggest as far as measuring and recording results is concerned, the only difference between NLP and CBT is that because we have no history of recording client feedback in a consistent and structured way or completing questionnaires to demonstrate progress, we do not have the evidence to be recognised by the National Institute for Health and Care Excellence (NICE).

At a very basic level, it would surely be simple to start collating this narrative evidence by monitoring the *before and after* progress of clients and then to record this information, with a variety of clients over a set time period. This would offer some evidence that your interventions have made a measurable difference.

Ellie Moseley, a recruitment consultant and NLP Practitioner, did just this as part of her modelling project. She modelled more successful recruitment consultants and noticed what they did to create their success (we know about modelling, so I don't need to explain further). She was able to obtain a sample of results that demonstrated similar behaviours across a range of successful consultants. Her findings were published in *Rapport* (Moseley, 2010) and weeks later, Ellie contacted me to say, 'As a result, things have really kicked off at work and I am really in demand with the training team'.

...so this worked well then.

Another important example of narrative evidence having an impact is through a case study done by Tracy Gray, an NLP Trainer who applied her extensive knowledge of the Healthcare system to a project she ran within the NHS Trust (Gray, 2019). The results of her work demonstrated a measurable impact and provide some powerful narrative evidence, demonstrating the efficacy of NLP, without the need for clinically robust research...and Tracey won two awards as a result of her project.

TIP

Start recording some of your own *before and after* scores for a range of interventions you undertake with clients. At least you are starting to gather some evidence of your effectiveness as an NLP Professional.

This may not be the robustness clinical research offers...and it is a start. It is one of many midway solutions between rigorous clinical evidence and nothing! Collecting narrative evidence to demonstrate what we do does work will start to bridge the gap between clinical research and the well-known, and unacceptable phrase 'well...it works'.

After all, I may not need to understand how my car works or what the mechanic has to do to keep it roadworthy, and I am obliged to obtain the evidence to demonstrate my car works before I can get insurance and use it on the road (it's called an MOT certificate). It is not good enough for me to simply tell the authorities my car works. I have to provide proof it still works, every year, before I can get my car tax.

Does NLP have standards?

It is fair to say that quite often, we avoid the topic of standards in NLP because we perceive these practices as potentially restrictive, stifling our flexibility, clipping our wings and denying us our natural leaning towards independent thinking and creativity. An NLP Trainer said to me just the other day: 'We are mavericks, we don't want to be governed by rules and standards.' Whilst I could respect that point of view and understand this is the attraction for some potential students, 'maverick' doesn't work for everyone! I wonder how well the maverick reputation works for those NLP Professionals who wish to attract clients who may be little more 'conventional'?

So, it is wise, at this point, to look at the difference between 'standards' and 'standardisation', because I think sometimes, the two are confused.

According to the Collins dictionary and thesaurus, a *standard* is a principle of propriety, honesty and integrity, a level of excellence or quality – something which presumably, all professionals would like to be associated with?

'Standardisation' on the other hand, is an attempt to regiment, i.e. to force discipline or order, especially in a domineering manner, which is both restrictive and stifling. This is something I personally would baulk at if applied to NLP and I am sure most other people would as well.

So, first of all, let's be clear: we do already have standards in NLP. For starters, the standards of professional practice as I referred to in Chapter 3. ANLP and other Associations already have a Code of Ethics and Complaints procedures and policies and standards for best practice – these are all standards for NLP. In fact, the Talking Circle of Associations I refer to , have created a unified Code of Ethics (Unified Code of Ethics, 2022) that can be adopted by any association and which demonstrates a commitment to best practice and ethics for NLP across the globe…as well as demonstrating the field of NLP is both unified and collaborative.

There are many areas where we appreciate the application of standards to practices and professions.

Probably the most well-known standard of practice is the Hippocratic Oath , which is commonly summed up as 'First do no harm' and was historically undertaken by physicians (although not actually required by many medical schools nowadays). Although this was written in the fifth century BC, it reflects a set of common principles for practice.

So acknowledging that NLP, through the independent NLP Associations, already has a common set of standards relating to best practice in NLP could create a greater sense of propriety, honesty and integrity within the profession and define a level of excellence or quality. Overtly supporting these standards and demonstrating that you practice within these does actually enhance your practice as an NLP Professional. Demonstrating your commitment to ongoing Professional Standards is going to enhance your reputation as an NLP Professional.

Are making a difference and making a living mutually exclusive?

Isn't it a well-known myth that only charlatans make money?

Isn't it also a myth that 'good' people who want to make a difference in the world cannot possibly enjoy the trappings of wealth, except in its 'purest' sense? Of course, it may be noble to believe I am wealthy because of all the riches I have in my life – friends, family, health, happiness – and that allegedly, these are the measures of true wealth rather than the fancy car and healthy bank balance. But, let's face it, they don't put food on the table or cover the monthly bills!

What if those beliefs were tweaked? What if the language was changed to 'I earn a living rather than make money and I am fortunate to do this in a field where making a difference is important.'

There are some people in the field, including me, who believed it was impossible to make a difference and make a living from NLP – the two were mutually exclusive and because I wanted to make a difference, I was destined to always be at the lower end of the financial scale. Now there is an interesting complex equivalence.

I even had evidence to support my belief. After all, I had witnessed friends who climbed up the financial ranks and lost their integrity and/or ethics. I had learned at an early age that/money doesn't buy happiness' and 'the love of money is the root of all evil' – those damned clichés again.

Indeed, I sat in a meeting of NLP leaders a couple of years ago and was questioned about the fact that I made a living from running ANLP. Even my sensory acuity picked up the indignant looks and expressions of surprise, and there were direct suggestions that running an association should be a voluntary role…even though I have no other form of income.

How that contrasted with a conversation I had with the former Community Interest Companies Regulator some years previously. As a relatively new CIC at the time, she had come to visit us and I was keen to point out that I didn't actually earn any money from running ANLP – it was a volunteer role that I did alongside my accountancy training business. She immediately corrected me and explained that running a social enterprise was a significant and responsible role and I should be receiving financial recompense for doing the job! It was another five years before I had built ANLP up enough to focus on it full time and even now, my income is a fifth of what I earned as an accounts trainer. That doesn't matter one bit because I enjoy what I do and feel that I am, at last, fulfilling my life purpose.

I am proud of the fact that ANLP is truly independent and isn't financially backed by any training company or consultancy practice, which means our loyalty is to our members.

Everyone, even those who believe their life purpose is to be in service to others, is entitled to exchange their services for something in return – usually money in our Western society though it could just as easily be bartering goods of services. To introduce an element of quantum physics, money is simply one form of energetic exchange between two people.

What if the new mantra for NLP Professionals could be:

'I will show up and I will serve…and what I do has to be attainable and sustainable.'

After all, how could I ever hope to make a consistent and sustainable difference to others if I am constantly worrying about putting the next meal on the table or keeping the roof over my head? I have a duty to ensure I balance the needs of others with my own needs because without that balance, serving others is neither attainable nor sustainable, which defeats the whole object of the exercise.

Believing that it is more than OK to earn a living whilst making a difference is a key step forward in dispelling this myth.

Does NLP Practitioner Training have to be a minimum 120 hours?

In the past, a division based upon the number of hours training evolved for a number of reasons, mainly because it was one of the few measures that existed in the earlier days of NLP. This resulted in clear divisions between NLP lineages, based upon the number of hours you have trained in order to obtain your NLP Practitioner certificate.

As long as I have been involved in NLP, there has been a debate around the number of hours one can train – 'full length' courses are around 20 days (120 hours) and 'shorter' courses can now be as short as 12 hours (yes, 12 hours!).

I could enter into a lengthy debate about the merits of shorter courses versus longer courses. To clarify, 12 hours is never going to be enough to develop the knowledge and skills required to become an NLP Professional.

However, I would respectfully suggest that this debate is really about so much more than the length of time one spends in a training room and this can no longer be the sole measure for the quality of an NLP course.

After all, all school students spend the same amount of time in school and yet they leave with a vast array of results, because it would be naive to suggest that their education depends solely on the length of time they spent in school! What about the quality of the teacher? The attitude of the student? The capabilities of the student (and teacher)? The teaching environment?

Within the education system, the quality of teaching is measured by the output of the students rather than the input of the teachers. In other words, schools are graded and assessed based upon the exam results and attainment levels achieved by their students. Apply this model to the field of NLP and the number of hours one spends in a training room become irrelevant – it's about what you can do as a result of spending time in a training room.

ANLP have been working on a project to develop nationally recognised and independently validated core competencies for NLP Training, which then leads directly into an established set of core competencies for NLP Professionals. I hope that by the time this book is published, there will be a breakthrough in this project and everyone will know about it.

When this happens, this advancement for the field of NLP will remove, once and for all, the long-held belief that quality NLP training can only be measured by the number of hours you have trained and focuses on output i.e. the knowledge and skills of the NLP Professional.

Does quality NLP training have to be face-to-face?

Once upon a time (perhaps up until March 2020) there was a firmly held belief in the NLP community that online training was bad. It was substandard and had to be avoided at all costs unless it was simply an introduction to NLP – an easy way to promote NLP and generate interest for a proper, face-to-face course.

Of course, the pandemic created an urgent need for greater flexibility and understanding as to what, specifically, defines a quality NLP training. The NLP community found itself catapulted into a situation where 'online' became essential.

And with that urgency, it became clear, very quickly, what was the difference that made the difference? It was less about the training room and more about the live, face-to-face elements of the training.

An online training had always been regarded as the type of training which involved watching a set of pre-recorded videos via an online platform…watch enough videos (sometimes as little as 12 hours' worth) and you get a practitioner certificate.

The key is that these particular types of online, pre-recorded video courses offer no interaction with a trainer or with other students, no opportunity to practice and no opportunity to receive feedback or have skills assessed.

These online courses within a training platform setting are more suited to subjects that are knowledge-based rather than those which have an element of skills-based subjective and experiential learning – and they do provide a great introduction to NLP.

NLP is subjective – I am confident we can all agree on this. Therefore, learning about NLP is subjective too and an NLP Professional does need to learn to apply the practical skills involved as well as absorb the theory-based knowledge.

Training provides the opportunity to assess both skills and knowledge, to build rapport and get to know your students, their capabilities, their values and beliefs, to observe their practice. There is a chance to mentor, guide, steer, advise and draw to attention things which may help or hinder a student striving to be the best NLP Professional they can possibly be.

So the key difference between an online training and a quality virtual training is the live, in-person element. The training has to be delivered live (even if it's via a virtual platform such as Zoom) and the students have to attend live at the same time as the training is being delivered (ie face-to-face).

This immediately offers the chance for flexibility, for interaction and questions, demonstrations and practice. It gives the trainer a chance to assess skills in the moment as well as test knowledge, so the subjective elements of NLP are maintained.

Of course, there are arguments that the practice elements may not delve so deeply in a virtual setting, as it's important to maintain safety and protect students from deep diving into a past trauma that is not suited to a training environment...and to be honest, dealing with more surface challenges is a safer place to be anyway as a student.

I recall my own Master Practitioner course, where I was supposed to be the coach in a breakthrough session. Having reviewed the personal history of my 'client' ie fellow student, I voiced my concerns about my ability to deal with things that may come up. I was assured that I would only be presented with things I could cope with, so I went ahead, despite my reservations – and my 'client' had a complete abreaction and left the building, with two trainers in hot pursuit.

Of course, maybe my reservations clouded my abilities on the day...and maybe I was presented with that experience because one day, that heightened awareness would be significant in my role, running the professional body for NLP. Whatever the reason, I have to say the experience did nothing for my confidence as an NLP student at the time and I wouldn't wish that on anyone as a new student to NLP.

So whether learning NLP in the same room or in a virtual space, it is important to understand that the challenges one addresses as part of the practice are more low level to start off with (3 out of 10 rather than 10 out of 10). Remember, medical students, wishing to specialise in neurosurgery begin with a simple procedure rather than being thrown in the deep end with a complex brain surgery.

The important and very significant learning over the last two years is that virtual training is possible and indeed has proved to be a successful alternative to training in the same physical space as your fellow students.

There are pros and cons to both and the field of NLP has benefitted from the evolution of training in the last couple of years. This particular genie – i.e. virtual training – is never going back in the bottle, so it was important to identify how quality training could still be delivered in a virtual setting.

The key answer to this question is yes, quality NLP training does have to be face-to-face. It is just the definition of what constitutes face-to-face that has evolved to include a virtual environment.

Is my Practitioner Certificate better than yours?

The greater challenge now that online and virtual trainings are competing in the same environment is helping the public to discern the difference between a quality NLP course and the 12-hour course available on some well known teaching platforms.

ANLP turn down more members on a weekly basis now due to Practitioners not realising that their 12-hour pre-recorded video based course is not sufficient to become an NLP Professional – and it is incumbent upon every person in the NLP community to share that same message, so that message becomes consistent, brighter and more widely heard.

Of course, it is confusing to the public that someone can obtain a practitioner certificate for completing an online course, when someone else can attend 120 hours face-to-face training and also obtain a Practitioner certificate. There is currently no discernible difference between the two given both people hold certificates entitling them to call themselves an 'NLP practitioner'.

It could be argued this diverse practice is not unique to the field of NLP because it is the same practice applied at universities too. The most prestigious universities in the UK (Oxford, Cambridge, and the other members of the Russell Group) offer the same undergraduate degree qualification as any of the second or even third tier universities i.e. Bachelor of Science (BSc or Batchelor of Arts (BA) – and now they can even charge the same tuition fees. Unless a graduate cites they have been to Oxford or Cambridge, most employers evaluate CVs based upon the class of degree rather than the where/how the degree was obtained – none of the employers I know have ever checked the University league tables when employing a graduate, especially as these change annually.

So yes, the currently system for obtaining a practitioner certificate through a short online training is misleading and unfair, and there is potential for further improvement (as my geography teacher would often write in my school report). Hence the work ANLP are doing on the core competencies project mentioned previously.

This happens in every evolving field of study, and the fact we are in a position to contribute to this continuing evolution is a cause for celebration. I believe every person in the NLP Community has the opportunity to contribute to and shape this evolution by the actions they take to promote their NLP training and explain the reasons these differences do make the difference.

Summary

We all have a vested interest in working together to develop the field of NLP into a more professional one. So apply whatever NLP techniques you have in your tool box to reframe and dispel any lingering myths you may have been holding on to or that you are faced with when promoting NLP to potential clients, so you can move forward with more confidence and commitment to the field of NLP.

Actions

- Consider which myths you may be holding on to – what is the purpose for that? What is the secondary gain for you by holding on to that myth?
- Use the reasoned reframes in this chapter to address any myths you come across when interacting with your potential clients?

CHAPTER 9
Shaping Your Future in NLP

'The best teamwork comes from men who are working independently toward one goal in unison.'
James Cash Penney, businessman and entrepreneur

At the end of the day, I understand you ultimately want your business to be more professional, effective and successful.

You want your investment in your NLP training, continuing professional development and business development to pay off and be worthwhile – you want a return on your investment (ROI).

You want to be recognised as a consummate NLP Professional, defined at the beginning of this book as 'A practitioner of NLP, who is serious about their business and who wants to make a difference by delivering their NLP services in a responsible, congruent and ethical way'.

Apart from the tips and actions scattered throughout this book, I have put together a list of recommended reading and resources you could choose to take on board and which would enable you to start creating the right mindset to develop a more professional, effective and successful NLP business.

Final thoughts...

It is easier than we realise, sometimes, to be the difference that makes a difference, and we all do make a difference to someone, every day. Remember, you cannot *not* communicate, and communicating does have an effect on others.

The smallest actions can sometimes have a knock-on effect and make a difference to the lives of others. You only have to think about the ripples which radiate across a pond when you throw one pebble into its centre. Every one of us is one of those pebbles, and our pond is everywhere – our home, our place of work, the supermarket, the cinema, the restaurant, or even the car park.

Once we have learned about NLP, we do use elements with varying degrees of unconscious competence. Sometimes, it is just our acceptance of the presuppositions of NLP which enables us to view things slightly differently and to take a more philosophical viewpoint.

Sometimes it is our understanding of the communication model, or our ability to naturally step into another person's shoes and see the world from their perspective. Whatever it is, our understanding does mean we are able to approach many situations in a different and more useful way. However we choose to apply our understanding of NLP, it does have an impact on our lives and the lives of others.

Think about the knock-on effect and greater social impact you could be having every day as you use your NLP to enrich the lives of others.

If this knock-on effect can happen so easily, it follows that we can also have unknown positive effects on others. Alan Briscoe was a Trainer with Mind Cymru's Positive Choices Project and he ran a two-day workshop called ASIST (Applied Suicide Intervention Skills Training). They provide practical training for caregivers seeking to prevent the immediate risk of suicide. So often in these situations, there is a reluctance to get involved for fear of making things worse, not knowing what to do, or just by assuming it is someone else's responsibility.

Alan received this feedback from someone who had completed his workshop:

> I wanted to let you know how much your training helped me today. I was on the train home from visiting my mother when I saw that the lady sitting opposite me was crying. Normally I wouldn't have said anything, scared that someone would think I was interfering, and as I sat there I kept remembering how on the ASIST course we had learned about how important it is to follow your gut instinct – I mean, she just looked so upset. So I started talking to her, and she didn't resent it at all, and seemed relieved to be able to talk to someone.

> When I asked her if she was thinking of killing herself, she just sat there nodding, for what seemed like ages and then looked at me and said thank you. In the past I would have been terrified of saying the wrong thing, and today I just followed what you showed us in the training. I felt really calm and focused on her.

> We carried on talking – of course, I missed my stop, and she really needed someone and today that was me. It has made me realise how locked away in our own lives we can be, and how amazing it is to be there for someone else, even a complete stranger. Anyway thank you again, the training was absolutely fabulous, best course I've ever been on – and today I might have just saved a life.

So, whether we know it or not, we are making a difference.

Go back to the secret NLP garden for a moment, and consider your own place within it. It doesn't matter if you choose to be a strawberry plant, a daffodil, or an oak tree. You can be the rope holding the garden swing, the cherub in the water fountain, or one of the succulent young carrots in the nursery bed.

It's a large garden, and whatever you choose to be within this garden, there is a place for you. And the thing which makes this garden so appealing is its diversity – there is something in it to appeal to everyone, even those who just want to come and sit for a while, and enjoy everything there is on offer.

The secret which makes this garden work so well is the way every element has its own identity, and yet works together and complements the other elements. Despite there being a great deal of diversity within it, there is a place for everything and everything has a place – and because of this, it means anyone coming into the garden can find what they are looking for, quickly and easily and start to enjoy what the NLP garden can offer them.

Remember the Decision Tree for a moment. This is where we can work together to make a difference in society – at the level where the public have a problem and want some options for helping them solve their problem.

You may think I am painting a rosy picture (no pun intended) and this view is too idealistic. We can continue to promote every flower, vegetable and feature as an individual unique aspect of a garden… and yet not many people notice one particular daffodil, however stunning it is.

Sometimes, to be noticed and make sure our beacon is shining brightly, we have to work together to make this bold and collective statement first – and the great thing about coalition is that it is about working together whilst maintaining our own identity.

I think sometimes that we forget the thing we all have in common — namely, that we all embrace and believe in NLP. It is NLP which hold us all together as a community, and gives us our place in this particular secret garden.

You could argue it is solely the responsibility of organisations like ANLP to increase that public awareness and make sure that more of the public do know about NLP. And I would agree with you ANLP does have a responsibility to inform and educate the public about NLP. ANLP also has a role in informing the public about all the benefits of NLP and the practical ways in which NLP can be used – and there are many.

And yet ANLP can only do this with your help, because at the end of the day, we are promoting your services to the public, not ours. So use ALL the resources available to you.

As I said earlier, it is my dream to get NLP recognised by the education system, partly because of this knock-on effect. Imagine the rippling social impact which could be made to primary school children when their teachers have a working knowledge and understanding of NLP. Imagine the difference which could be made to secondary school students when they experience some of the positive impact of NLP for themselves. Imagine how this could help with their confidence levels at exam time or during interviews, for starters.

Imagine the knock-on effect of this social impact on society in a few years time, when every person leaving school has heard of and experienced NLP. This would mean an understanding of NLP would go with these students into their careers, wherever this may be — and so when these organisations are approached by an NLP practitioner in the future, there will already be someone within who can support the value of your work based on their own experience at school.

By adopting the principles laid out in this book, we can all play a part in ensuring there is a successful, professional, responsible element within the field of NLP.

This field will only get the recognition it deserves when we are proud to associate ourselves with quality NLP rather than dressing it up as something else, in an attempt to dissociate from the minority of poor NLP Practitioners.

At the moment, NLP is at a crossroads. We have the opportunity to shape the future for our profession and decide on the course we want NLP to take in the future – the power lies with us, as NLP Professionals, to make this happen.

We love NLP and we know what a difference it makes, so it's time to take back ownership of quality NLP and use it to shape our future in NLP.

References

Advertising Standards Authority Home Page. (2022, Feb 03). Retrieved from Advertising Stndards Authority: https://www.asa.org.uk/

Almond, N. (2019, Dec 17). *The Anatomy of a Plane Crash*. Retrieved from ANLP International CIC: https://anlp.org/case-studies/the-anatomy-of-a-plane-crash

ANLP Complaints Policy. (2020, Mar 01). Retrieved from ANLP International CIC: https://anlp.org/anlp-complaints-policy

ANLP Criteria for Virtual Training. (2020, Jun 01). Retrieved from ANLP International CIC: https://anlp.org/anlp-criteria-for-virtual-training

ANLP Members Code of Ethics. (2019, Dec 17). Retrieved from ANLP International CIC: https://anlp.org/anlp-members-code-of-ethics

Armson, P. D. (2016). *Enough? How Much Money Do You Need For The Rest of Your Life?* CreateSpace Independent Publishing.

ASA Guidelines for ANLP Members. (2019, Dec 17). Retrieved from ANLP International CIC: https://anlp.org/knowledge-base/asa-guidelines

ASA Testimonials and Endorsements. (2022, Feb 03). Retrieved from Adertising Standards Authority: https://www.asa.org.uk/advice-online/testimonials-and-endorsements.html

Bitesize Video Resources. (2020, May 01). Retrieved from ANLP International CIC: https://anlp.org/bitesize-video-resources

Bong, L. (2018, Oct 28). The Value of Accreditation. *Rapport 60*, pp. 52-53.

Brown, B. (2015). *Rising Strong.* Vermillion.

Churches, R. A. (2007). *NLP for Teachers: how to be a highly effective teacher.* Crown House Publishing.

Collaborating Associations. (2020, Jun 01). Retrieved from ANLP International CIC: https://anlp.org/collaborating-associations

Definition of Myth. (2022, Feb 03). Retrieved from Cambridge Dictionary: https://dictionary.cambridge.org/dictionary/english/myth

Dilts, R. B. (2015). *Next Generation Entrepreneurs: Live Your Dreams and Create a Better World Through Your Business (Success Factor Modeling): 1.* . Dilts Srategy Group.

Dr de Rijk, L. (2021, Apr 8). *Reconsolidation of Traumatic Memories, an NLP-based Protocol for PTSD treatment.* Retrieved from ANLP Internaitonal CIC: https://anlp.org/ blog/reconsolidation-of-traumatic-memories-an-nlp-based-protocol-for-ptsd-treatment

Dr Parker, P. E. (2021). CBT Repackaged or a novel treatment? The Lightning Process compared with UK specialist medical care for pedeatric Chronic Fatigue Syndrome. *Fatigue: Biomedicine, Health and Behaviour 9.*

Dunlop, M. M. (2020, Apr 01). *Introduction to Resilience and Wellbeing for Social Care Workers.* Retrieved from You Tube: https://www.youtube.com/watch?v=JwNlT-JpOag&t=5s

Falconer, K. (2021, Jun 01). *NLP from the Heart.* Retrieved from ANLP International CIC: https://anlp.org/news/nlp-from-the-heart

Fielding, G. (2008). My daughter wanted a pet, so I bought her a greyhound. *My daughter wanted a pet, so I bought her a greyhound.* Nightingale Conant.

Gerber, M. E. (2001). *The E-Myth Revisited: why most small businesses don't work and what to do about it.* Harper Collins.

Gray, T. (2019, Dec 17). *Changing Attitudes, Improving Outcomes – A case study of NLP interventions in the NHS.* Retrieved from ANLP International CIC: https://anlp.org/case-studies/changing-attitudes-improving-outcomes-a-case-study-of-an-nlp-intervention-in-the-nhs

Henwood, S. A. (2007). *NLP and Coaching for Healthcare Professionals: developing expert practice.* John Wiley and Sons.

How to Apply for Professional Standards (2020, Sep 01). Retrieved from ANLP International CIC: https://anlp.org/knowledge-base/how-to-apply-for-professional-standards

McNally, E. (2021, Apr 28). TPP and NLP. *Rapport 70,* pp. 10-12. Retrieved from https://anlp.org/rapport/read/lite/rapport-70---spring-2021

Menezes-Cunningham, E. (2009, Jun 28). How being extra helpful can be good for business. *Rapport18,* pp. 20-22.

Moseley, E. (2010, Jan 28). Modelling Skills in Recruitment. *Rapport 18,* pp. 40-41.

NLP Awards. (2017, Apr 29). Retrieved from NLP Awards: https://www.nlpawards.com

NLP Certification Structure. (2019, Dec 17). Retrieved from ANLP INternational CIC: https://anlp.org/knowledge-base/nlp-certification-structure

NLP Information and Research. (2022, Feb 03). Retrieved from NLP Wiki: http://nlpwiki.org/wiki

NLP International Conference. (2016, May 01). Retrieved from NLP International Conference: https://www.nlpconference.com

NLP Research Papers. (2019, Dec 17). Retrieved from ANLP International CIC: https://anlp.org/knowledge-base/nlp-research-papers

Oxford Online Dictionary. (2022, Feb 02). Retrieved from Oxford Online Dictionary: https://www.oxforddictionaries.com

Presuppositions of NLP. (2019, Dec 17). Retrieved from ANLP International CIC: https://anlp.org/knowledge-base/presuppositions-of-nlp

Research and Recognition Project Home Page. (2022, Feb 03). Retrieved from R and R Project: https://randrproject.org/

Seymour, J. (2009, Mar 28). The Seven Practices of Transformational NLP. *Rapport 15*, pp. 32-35.

Social media profiles that ruined job offers. (2022, Feb 03). Retrieved from Total Jobs: https://www.totaljobs.com/advice/the-job-academy-social-media-profiles-that-ruined-job-offers

Social Proof. (2022, Feb 03). Retrieved from Wikipedia: https://en.wikipedia.org/wiki/Social_proof

The Importance of Client Reviews. (2020, May 01). Retrieved from ANLP International CIC: https://anlp.org/blog/the-importance-of-client-reviews

Tosey, P. A. (2009). *Neuro-Linguistic-Progamming: a critical apprecaition for manageers and developers.* Palgrave Macmillan.

Tversky, A. A. (1973). A heuristic for judging frequency and probability. *Cognitive Psychology Vol 5, Issue 2.*

UK Government Legislation. (2022, Feb 03). Retrieved from Legislation.gov.uk: https://www.legislation.gov.uk

UKCP Standards of Education and Training. (2022, Feb 03). Retrieved from UK Council for Psychotherapy: https://www.psychotherapy.org.uk/ukcp-members/standards-guidance-and-policies/

Unified Code of Ethics. (2022, Feb 28). Retrieved from Unified NLP Home Page: https://www.unifiednlp.org/

Further Reading

Cheal, Melody, 'How Supervision Adds Value to NLP', *Rapport 72*, pp.46-48
https://anlp.org/media/Resources/Rapport%20Articles/
Business%20Development%2072%20Supervision%20
Melody%20Cheal%2046.pdf?_t=1635420929

Chödrön, Pema, *Living Beautifully with Uncertainty and Change.*
Shambhala Publications, 2019.

Coley, Andy Using NLP in the NHS Case Study:
https://anlp.org/case-studies/using-nlp-in-the-nhs

Forleo, Marie *Everything is Figureoutable.*
Portfolio Penguin, 2019.

Lee, Aileen, Social Proof is the New Marketing:
https://techcrunch.com/2011/11/27/social-proof-why-people-
like-to-follow-the-crowd/

McKeown, Greg *Essentialism.*
Virgin Books, 2014.

McLachlan, John & Meager, Karen Time Mastery
Panoma Press, 2017

Self, Jonathan, *Good Money, Become an Ethical Entrepreneur.*
Head of Zeus Ltd, 2017.

Resources

To access free additional resources to include the templates, sub-scribe at: www.thenlpprofessional.com

Simple Business Plan Template
Executive summary
Vision
The business idea
Running the business
Business goals
What the business does
What makes the business different
SWOT Analysis
Key Personnel & Staff
Finance
Start-up costs
Profit and loss forecast
Sourcing finance
Managing financial risks
Sales and marketing
Market research
Managing market risks
Pricing
Promotion and advertising

Case Studies Template – reproduced by kind permission of ANLP

Category
e.g. Fears and phobias, anxiety, weight loss, confidence, parenting, business, health etc

Catchy Title (10 words)
Something that captures attention and entices someone to click and read your case study

CHALLENGE

What was the presenting challenge/problem (200 words max)?
Please include what else had they tried before choosing NLP?

How did the challenge effect the client (200 words max)?
Please include their words, their behaviours, their feelings about the challenge…what did they see, what did they hear, what did they feel, what did they know? What else had they tried before choosing NLP?

NLP SOLUTION

What did you do to empower your client to move forward and make the changes they wanted (200 words max)?
Please explain, succinctly, how the sessions worked, what does a session look like, sound like, feel like…so a potential client understands what happens during an NLP session. How many hours/sessions did the client need with you?

RESULT

What did the client say about their experience (200 words max)?
What changed for the client? What did they do differently afterwards? What happened next time they met with the challenge? How did this impact on their life?

Any Other Business Podcast – Rob Bence and Rob Dix:
https://aob.show/
For Insights into running a growing business

Companies House: https://www.gov.uk/government/
organisations/companies-house
For information on company structures look at the business and self-employed section and the tools and guidance for business.

Factotum: https://ukfactotum.com/
Phone answering service used by ANLP for many years.

HM Revenue and Customs: https://www.gov.uk/government/
organisations/hm-revenue-customs
For advice on all aspects of UK taxation, VAT and employers' obligations.

Intellectual Property Office: https://www.gov.uk/government/
organisations/intellectual-property-office
For information about protecting your own intellectual property.

UK Government Advice: https://www.gov.uk/working-for-yourself
for advice about setting up your own business.

Summary of Actions

1. **Adopting a professional attitude**

   Choose one of these areas to work on in the next three months:

   - Create or review your business plan.

   - Allocate some quality time in your diary to work 'on' your business.

   - Review your personal appearance as an NLP Professional and choose one aspect to improve.

   Whichever area you choose, make sure you create at least one SMART goal…and email me on admin@anlp.org when you have completed your goal.

2. **Being congruent with what you do**

   - Choose any NLP strategy and apply it to your business. You have plenty to choose from including well-formed outcomes, the presuppositions of NLP, perceptual positions, pacing and leading, cause and effect.

   - Re-elicit your business values and prioritise them – check these against both your personal values and your business plan and make sure all aspects align.

3. **Demonstrating best practice**

- If you haven't already got them, create one-to=-one coaching agreements for your clients – these will protect both you and them in the event of any misunderstanding.

- Commit to at least one continual professional development (CPD) activity in the next three months. This can be anything from attending a practice group meeting to booking a business workshop/webinar or reading a relevant book.

4. **Appreciating the value of social proof**

- Collect testimonials from your next three clients and use them on your website and in your promotional materials (NB Make sure they comply with CAP guidelines).

- Join a Professional Body or Trade Association. It would be great if this was ANLP...and any professional membership will add to your social proof.

5. **Celebrating the Diversity of NLP**

    Identify your niche market, by asking yourself the following questions:

- What is your potential niche?

- What problems could your potential niche possibly solve?

- Why do these problems continue?

- Who do you most enjoy working with?

6. **Working collaboratively**

- Make contact with and introduce yourself to at least one other NLP Professional in your local area. Just be curious and be open to the possibilities that might arise when you explore potential avenues for working collaboratively.

7. **Raising awareness of NLP**

Write at least one success story which is relevant to your niche and use this to promote your services and obtain some extra PR via local media (radio, magazines and newspapers). Remember to send it in to *Rapport* magazine too for inclusion in a future issue of the magazine for NLP Professionals!

8. **Dispelling Some Common Myths in NLP**

- Consider which myths you may be holding on to – what is the purpose for that? What is the secondary gain for you by holding on to that myth?

- Review your marketing and promotional materials and make sure you are acknowledging NLP in your literature – be the change you want to see in your world.

Acknowledgements

I have many people to thank, who have all supported me in my life and in my role as CEO of ANLP.

To my ANLP colleagues, Ambassadors, Specialist Envoys, Council of Generative Wisdom and Volunteers, for their unwavering support, wisdom and guidance as we walk this path together.

To all the people mentioned in this book and all NLP Professionals, especially members of ANLP, who are out there, making a difference every day…without you, there would be no purpose.

To those who gave us this gift called NLP, Richard Bandler, John Grinder and Frank Pucelik, and the ANLP Honorary Fellows – Connirae Andreas, Judith DeLozier, Robert Dilts, Charles Faulkner, Stephen Gilligan, Christina Hall, L Michael Hall, Tad James, Bill O'Hanlon, Julie Silverthorn, and Wyatt Woodsmall.

To all the NLP Professionals I have had the privilege to meet and work with, including Joe and Melody Cheal, Clare Church, Andy Coley, Andy Coote, Mark Deacon, Judith DeLozier, Robert Dilts, Tim and Kris Hallbom, Suzanne Henwood, Jeremy Lazarus, Judith Lowe, Ian McDermott, Tony Nutley, Julie Silverthorn, Paul Tosey and Reb Veale. Many of these NLP companions generously give their time, knowledge and understanding to be there for me and ANLP and I am truly grateful for their support.

To my Talking Circle of Associations colleagues, Bert Feustal (INLPTA), Ueli R. Frischknecht (IANLP), and Karl and Nandana Nielsen (IN-Institutes).

To Pauline Newman and Kathy Strong, who first introduced me to NLP and unknowingly gave me the signposts for what continues to be an amazing journey.

To my wider family – my dad, who passed away too young; my mum and my brother, who challenge me daily and love me fiercely and to my Auntie Coral, who has always believed in me.

Most importantly, to my immediate family – who are my reasons for being. My two boys, Tom and Daniel, for their unwavering faith and patience, which has enabled me to be both a mum and a Professional; my daughter-in-law, Shannen, who is the daughter I never had; my two beautiful grandchildren, Edward and Emily who teach me the true meaning of presence and bring me joy; my stepsons, Ben and Jamie, who embraced and accepted me when I became part of their extended family…and my husband, Kash, who has supported me and encouraged me to shine my light – thank you!

About the Author

Karen Falconer is the CEO of the Association for NLP, the global flagbearers for Professional NLP, an independent, award-winning social enterprise specialising in membership services for NLP Professionals. She is motivated to do the best she can to help NLP become more credible, so it will be embraced by the education system and will positively influence more young people to achieve their full potential.

As well as running ANLP, the NLP International Conference and the NLP Awards, Karen is the editor of *Rapport*, the magazine for NLP Professionals, and the publisher of *Acuity* and the NLP Research Journal, *Current Research in NLP*.

She was Chair of Trustees (School Governor) at her local Secondary School Academy and was part of the Developing Special Provision Locally Parent Reference group for Hertfordshire County Council. She was awarded Hertfordshire Woman of the Year in the 2009 Hertfordshire Business Awards.

Karen occasionally blogs about her personal reflections on life and when she has spare time, she enjoys singing in The London Show Choir, as well as painting, reading, crafts, the theatre and watching (not participating in!) sports, especially rugby.

Karen and Kash married in Italy in 2018 and they live in Hertfordshire with their dog, cat and youngest son (when he is not at university). Between them, Karen and Kash have four amazing, grown-up boys and two beautiful grandchildren (so far!).

Karen can be contacted by email via admin@anlp.org

www.thenlpprofessional.com

www.anlp.org

www.nlpconference.com

www.nlpawards.com

"And as we let our own light shine, we unconsciously give other people permission to do the same."
Marianne Williamson, *A Return to Love: Reflections on the Principles of 'A Course in Miracles'*